NEW CLOTHES
FOR THE OLD MAN

By
C. F. WIMBERLY

First Fruits Press
Wilmore, Kentucky
c2016

New clothes for the old man.
By C. F. Wimberly.

First Fruits Press, ©2016
Previously published by the Pentecostal Publishing Co., [193-?].

ISBN: 9781621715443 (print) 9781621715450 (digital) 9781621715467 (kindle)

Digital version at http://place.asburyseminary.edu/firstfruitsheritagematerial/130/

First Fruits Press is a digital imprint of the Asbury Theological Seminary, B.L. Fisher Library. Asbury Theological Seminary is the legal owner of the material previously published by the Pentecostal Publishing Co. and reserves the right to release new editions of this material as well as new material produced by Asbury Theological Seminary. Its publications are available for noncommercial and educational uses, such as research, teaching and private study. First Fruits Press has licensed the digital version of this work under the Creative Commons Attribution Noncommercial 3.0 United States License. To view a copy of this license, visit http://creativecommons.org/licenses/by-nc/3.0/us/.

For all other uses, contact:

First Fruits Press
B.L. Fisher Library
Asbury Theological Seminary
204 N. Lexington Ave.
Wilmore, KY 40390
http://place.asburyseminary.edu/firstfruits

Wimberly, C. F. (Charles Franklin), 1866-1946.

   New clothes for the old man / by C.F. Wimberly. Wilmore, Kentucky : First Fruits Press, ©2016.

   219 pages, [1] leaf of plates : portrait ; 21 cm.

   Reprint. Previously published: Louisville, Ky. : Pentecostal Publishing Co., [193-?].

   ISBN: 9781621715443 (paperback)

   1. Sanctification. I. Title.

BT765 .W55 2016

Cover design by Jonathan Ramsay

asburyseminary.edu
800.2ASBURY
204 North Lexington Avenue
Wilmore, Kentucky 40390

First Fruits Press
The Academic Open Press of Asbury Theological Seminary
204 N. Lexington Ave., Wilmore, KY 40390
859-858-2236
first.fruits@asburyseminary.edu
asbury.to/firstfruits

C. F. Wimberly, B. A.

NEW CLOTHES FOR THE OLD MAN.

BY

C. F. WIMBERLY, B. A.

PENTECOSTAL PUBLISHING CO.,
LOUISVILLE, KY.

DEDICATORY

To the precious men and women everywhere who believe in the utmost efficacy of the Blood; some whose unselfish love has been a break-water to me in times of sorrow and crisis; others whose kindly interest and Spirit-filled ministry have helped and encouraged me so much, this volume is lovingly dedicated by the

AUTHOR.

THE MAN AND THE BOOK.

Rev. C. F. Wimberly contributes another book on the all-important subject of *sin*, and how to get rid of it. He is a gifted writer, a successful pastor, with evangelistic fire burning in him. There are few young men in our Methodism in whom the pastor and the evangelist is so well combined. He holds most successful revivals in his church, and as pastor, conserves and develops the good results of his protracted efforts. He is a university man, has been a hard student, and had the advantage of wide reading.

He writes also from experience—he has known what it was to war with the Old Man, and has experienced that deliverance from indwelling sin, which can be wrought only by the Holy Spirit. So he writes not only from a scriptural and theoretical, but also from an experimental knowledge of the subject under discussion. He treats an old subject in a new and unique fashion. He attacks the "Old Man" in his best guise, and uncovers him in his most ingenious disguise.

The book is written in attractive style, the points are clear and forcefully put, and the conclusions are brought home with a forcefulness that can but make an impression upon the mind of the reader. We bespeak for the book a wide reading, and pray that its message may reach and bless many hearts, and that it may be the means of bringing many souls into a full deliverance from the remains of the carnal mind.

H. C. MORRISON.

PREFACE

The wisest man who ever lived said nearly three thousand year ago " of making many books there is no end." No doubt that great mind was overwhelmed by ponderous volumes, and his inability to "keep up" with the new productions. Such a thought in comparison with the book question of this generation is somewhat amusing. To become familiar with the titles of present day books, alone, not to mention the reading of them, would be a task beyond the mental and physical powers of any man.

We are conscious that it requires courage to launch a new book and risk its chances among the millions already written and the thousands coming to the light annually. Why not stop? Is it not time? Why are books written? There are obvious reasons: Some are written to satisfy and enlarge a literary fame or reputation for scholarship; others are written for pastime, and to be read for the same reason;

and still others for revenue only. They have no message, their readers do not want any. It is money on one hand and a morbid appetite on the other. At opposite extremes there are two other classes of books; the one written under the unctious glow of the Holy Spirit, inspiration is too strong a word. Such books are conceived of motives as high and holy as a Gospel sermon; they may be poetry, fiction, or discussions on theological doctrines. The other class, we believe, to be truly conceived and written under satanic unction, with motives fresh from the Pit; they wither and blight whatsoever they touch. This gulf-stream of iniquity will continue to widen and deepen. Hence, there should be no apology for a good book. We can never hope to preach a *new* Gospel that will be in harmony with the Bible, but we can give the Old Gospel a new setting and a better viewpoint.

Just as the field, for fresh gospel truth, is inexhaustible, so is the place for fresh books on old themes inexhaustible. My first conception of the "Old Man," or Original Sin, was exhumed from dry theologies at the seminary. I looked upon it as a theological curio, to be studied like the bi-nominal theorem, not for practical value, but that I may pass the seminary and conference examinations. That this *something* was a vital throbbing agency in every human life I had but a vague idea. Theological scholarship will give us an abstract knowledge of our depraved nature, but the *sanctifying grace of the Holy Spirit will give us a concrete* EPIGNOSIS *of our "Old Man."* Many diversions, make-believes, and pretenses of human conduct, as seen in social, commercial, and religious life can never be understood until the *carnal mind* is brought into the lime-light of Holy Ghost illumination. The reader is asked to keep in mind the irony used througout the book; otherwise it will seem to be a jumbled argument on both sides of the question. Praying sincerely that my humble service may prove a blessing to many hearts that I shall not meet until the Judgment, and asking each reader to remember the writer at the mercy Throne, I send this little volume as Bread cast upon the waters.

Louisville, Ky.

CONTENTS.

Page

CHAPTER I.
In Which His Measure Is Being Taken.. 17

CHAPTER II.
In Which Some Close Fitting Is Observed. 25

CHAPTER III.
In Which the Details of Further Fitting Is Secured 33

CHAPTER IV.
In Which the Texture of an Outer Garment Is Examined................ 41

CHAPTER V.
In Which the Color Receives Due Attention 49

CHAPTER VI.
In Which the Beauty Is Seen at a Distance 57

CHAPTER VII.
In Which the Cash Values are Considered 65

CHAPTER VIII.
In Which the Size of Garments Is Studied. 73

CHAPTER IX.
In Which Practical Styles Are Recommended 81

CHAPTER X.
In Which Cleaning and Pressing Is Urged 89

CHAPTER XI.
In Which the Clothing Is Up-To-Date For Place and Season. 97

CHAPTER XII.
In Which Views of a Particular Style are Freely Expressed. 105

A Pen Sketch with a Warning. 113

IN WHICH HIS MEASURE IS TAKEN

NEW CLOTHES FOR THE OLD MAN

By C. F. Wimberly, B. A.

CHAPTER I

IN WHICH HIS MEASURE IS TAKEN.

The term "Old man" is Biblical, and even a superficial study of the origin and history of what it stands for, will show how eminently fitting is this odd title. A misunderstanding of the significance of this subtle warp in human character is the basis of all the modern controversy on the lines of personal salvation. An understanding will both clarify and fortify us from a continuation of an unfortunate polemical war.

The theological pros and cons of the subject have been so thoroughly analyzed, aired, and thrashed out by able writers and preachers in and out of the holiness movement that we do not deem it necessary to undertake any new exploration in that realm. Such a method will settle the question in about the same way that the mode of baptism has been settled. There are numerous terms used by the Scriptures to designate the Old Man, viz: "man of sin," "root of bitterness," "carnal mind," etc.; the theologians call it depravity, original sin, or a moral bent to evil. All these words represent that *pollution* which has fallen as an inheritance to the entire human race, marvelously affecting body, mind, and soul. The effect of this dreadful desecration is that the innate tendency of the entire race is only evil and that continually. No one is immune. So strange and powerful is this *something* within us, drawing by cables fastened into the inmost soul, that it seems to be a real personality, or another *self*. To deny such an existence is to advertise ignorance of God's word, and our own selves. It is a fact that human nature gravitates to evil, and such a fact can not be a happen-so; this is not a world of chance.

We hear much these days about the great "brotherhood" and "fatherhood" questions; ministers of Christ talking and writing about the element of good that should be recognized and cultivated in all religions; ethical culture that should play such a prominent part in the church's campaign for the world. It all sounds well and reads well, but the so-called natural religion is a humbug. There may be natural religion, but there is no such thing as natural salvation. We often see splendid examples of moral uprightness in those who make no profession of saving faith, but such examples are due to the reflex influence of the Christian standards. To put the cause elsewhere is to rob Jesus Christ of glory that is His own. Our desire is to throw some side-lights on the character of the Old Man; and he is an adept at assuming and presuming with a beautiful exterior for capital, when the real thing contains the germ of every sin in the decalogue; a cage of every unclean and hateful thing.

Much light has been thrown on this supposed mysterious theological subject by recent Holy Ghost writers who have exhumed it from ponderous documents, where it had been fossilized for centuries. It is now no longer a dry bone to be examined and explained by theories, like a prehistoric fowl; but a living issue, a dreadful enemy which the learned and unlearned alike must meet and grapple to the death. The unsophisticated peasant of to-day, who has discovered this incarnated traitor, knows far more than the scholarly theologian of yesterday. The Old Man's satanic genius has been marvelously revealed in his ability to keep out of sight, knowing that it would be dangerous to be discovered. But, like the beautiful maiden that was given to Alexander the Great by a king whom he had captured, all the hideousness, moral and spiritual poison may be hidden by amiable characteristics that may have all the appearances of the good and true. This legendary maiden had been fed on poison from childhood, so that her touch, her breath, her embrace, meant certain death. We should be as cunning as the great conqueror, who beneath the graceful form, rosy cheeks, smiling lips, and lovely eyes, located the trap that was set for his destruction. The very caption of these papers, when first written, Ethical and Aesthetical Side of the Old Man, sounds paradoxical, but we want to locate him in his most subtle and dangerous role.

The Old Man made his *debut* into the affairs of human life when the first pair roamed in pristine purity through the glories of their earthly paradise. He became rooted and grounded in the soul-fiber of the federal head of the race, and the whole stream of life has been polluted from that hour. He has been no respecter of persons; no race, tongue, or kindred has escaped. No fact, material or immaterial, is more certain than the existence of this moral blight so aptly named by the Apostle Paul. In whomsoever the Old Man remains and has not been "crucified" or "put off" through faith in the blood, Satan has a playground, or in modern naval parlance, a coaling station. In the soil of this peculiar spot found in every heart are sin germs, either dormant or growing against all the moral law. The actual transgressions of the human race are governed by environment, opportunity, or rigid discipline and not by good, better, best, seen among men.

Thousands of the knowing sort deny the real existence of our Old Man, and this denial plays a prominent part in popular theology.

New Clothes for the Old Man.

Definite conclusions have been reached by well arranged arguments and laws of logic. The devil is never so well pleased as when men declare his non-existence; likewise the Old Man is *de-lighted* to have himself reasoned out, and he will do even better, he will aid in the processes of his own annihilation.

IN WHICH SOME CLOSE FITTING
IS OBSERVED.

CHAPTER II

IN WHICH SOME CLOSE FITTING IS OBSERVED.

The Bible is our great encyclopedia of divine knowledge and from its pages, the preached word, and even the study of the theologies, we may learn much about our original sin, depravity, etc.; but we will never really know our Old Man until we get interested in the Fountain that was opened in the long ago for sin and uncleanness. The struggling soul will then discover a *war*, and a bitter protest to every inch of advancement and every item of consecration.

It is amusing to see how very interested the Old Man is to have the revival begin, and how he rejoices to see certain loved ones and neighbors getting right with God, but the first gun that is fired toward him will mean that Fort Sumpter has been fired on, and war is now declared. The smiles, nodding approval, the hand-shaking so conspicuous in the early part of the meeting are seen no more.

No one can be more anxious to show real interest in the promotion of every good cause as our venerable companion, but it must be done in decency and order; perfect decorum should always characterize our movement. Anything violent or radical is very shocking to his nerves. The quiet anxious seat, or inquiry room is far more preferable than the "mourner's bench" and straw carpet. We shall examine this special phase more fully in the future.

It is true, however, that among the many and exhaustive discussions on this great theme, the most subtle and harmful characteristics of the Old Man have been more or less overlooked except a gleam here and there. Satan is never so dangerous and destructive as when he plays the roll of an "Angel of Light." The horns and hoofs would be very detrimental and embarrassing to his majesty, if well advertised and known.

The Old Man never towers so high in might and wisdom as when he assumes the roll of *esthetical lady* or *ethical, cultured gentleman.* There are human monstrosities and incarnate devils, as a result of Satan having full swing with our depraved natures, but when the earthly, sensual, and devilish mind parades in the metamorphoser of the accomplished and refined, the influence becomes nothing less than a sirocco of death borne on the wings of an evening zephyr.

It is the purpose of this book to show some side lights on this extraordinary twist in our nature, for which we seem to be irresponsible and responsible for its presence and conduct. We feel sure that when once the flashlight of God's truth is thrown on the Old Man, and he is discovered—also the method or remedy for his removal, responsibility for his existence will begin. There is so much beautiful foliage clustered about that the real fruit of worm-wood is obscured.

The first one we shall mention is Ambition. At once arguments pile up in favor of this necessary passion. The great work of the world could not progress without it. Great achievements, enterprises, and inventions could never be but for noble ambition. What is more commendable than a real zeal to get there—forge to the front—to be in the public eye as a capable leader? Nothing is so toothsome as a stirring appeal that will stimulate and arouse latent energies to lead the procession.

A minister should leave no stone unturned in qualifying himself for great usefulness. There are plenty to work in the narrow, humbler spheres, but only a few who can minister to the larger interests of the church. Covet the best gifts. Certainly. Everything belonging to a broad education: Science, philosophy, literature, elocution, and when possible, travel. To be *useful*, we must be eligible and acceptable with the educated and cultured. Voice, gesture, rhetoric, and position should be studied and mastered. Truth becomes transfigured and powerful if all the laws of public address are observed. It is not only what is said but every one should not fail to observe *how* it was said. The call is coming up continually for cultivated men who can draw crowds, in other words the opening is for *stars*.

Failing to observe this modern trend of thought and demand is sure to relegate one to the rear and forever close doors that are ready to open for those prepared to enter. It is beautiful sentiment and poetry: "the flowers that are born to blush unseen, and waste their sweetness on the desert air," but it should not be, we must make full proof of our ministry.

There are many clever ways that pious ambition may get itself on the great world market. Nothing is so startling as to be suddenly called upon for an address; unexpected, of course, therefore unprepared—innuendo apologies are in order, feigned embarrassment, etc. Then proceed to deliver with sophomoric swing and jingle material thoroughly prepared and committed before. This method never fails to produce a profound impression. "What could he do if only prepared?" The Old Man is delighted.

In all other vocations the same spirit should be crystallized into a living, throbbing purpose to achieve honor and greatness. Be a captain of industry. If it is in the political realm, time, money, and personal effort should be given a willing sacrifice to the common good. There are laws to be enacted, financial leakage to be stopped, wrongs righted. Who are to do those things? Ask the Old Man.

IN WHICH THE DETAILS OF FURTHER FITTING IS SECURED.

CHAPTER III

IN WHICH THE DETAILS OF FURTHER FITTING IS SECURED.

Another side light on the Old Man is that he enjoys very much to have the reputation for being *broad* and *liberal*. Nothing stultifies character so much as subscribing to the narrow views of others. We are not living in the eighteenth or even the nineteenth centuries, but the twentieth; and there is nothing narrow about this age. The view-point reaches out and beyond the creeds, customs, and superstitions of the past. If we are "heirs of all the centuries," why not utilize them, and avoid the fog and fogyism that kept our forefathers in darkness? The only gospel that can meet and satisfy present day demands must be humanitarian, cosmopolitan, and, above all, ethical and practical.

The cry is heard throughout the land, the church is not reaching the men. Why? The reason is obvious; men *think* these days. How can man who has awakened to a consciousness of his wonderful ego ever submit to the vague, intangible tenets of yesterday's mysticism? Never. If men could hear something worthy of their majestic conceptions of God, the Universe, and soul-power, the churches would be packed. Orthodoxy served its day and generation, and did it well, but now its place is in the ecclesiastical archives, and should be examined with veneration due all branches of sacred history.

The Old Man hails the incoming of a new theology. Our next "great awakening" must come along lines of advanced thought. The additional light that has come through the study of psychology gives strong evidence against trying to maintain the antiquated doctrines of repentance, faith, and salvation by a blood atonement. No more slaughter-house theology for the Old Man. The experiences of salvation so real to our fathers can now be explained by psychological laws. The agonies of repentance, and the necessity of restitution, the old *mourner's bench* were necessary then, because of a prevailing custom; now such things are

New Clothes for the Old Man. 35

ridiculous, but for the fact many humble, sincere souls pratice them. No one has ever understood the philosophy of conversion, and modern teachers should know better than to undertake an explanation. Children are brought in through the Sunday-school, and Epworth League, so that the plan of salvation is simplified for the comprehension of any child.

The Old Man is a strong believer in "Decision Day," which will, if adopted by all the Sunday-schools mark the beginning of a new era in revivalism. The older and more obstinate sinners could be easily handled in the "Inquiry Room" annex to the evangelical meetings. The church and pastor who can not adjust themselves to the present situation is doomed and ought to be.

To confess Christ in some quiet place is so simple and easy. All the embarrassment and humiliation of sin and guilt are eliminated. The best scholarship has discovered that travail of soul on account of some future impending woe is a delusion. A religious renaissance is now blessing our time honored shores, and the preacher who has not so read the signs of the times should be staked out on Brushby creek, a place where he can not impose on the feelings of our cultured, fastidious congregations. Water seeks its level so does the preacher. The fortifications of sin are not so grim and Gibraltar-like as we have always understood; such ideas, with scores of similar ones, have grown out of a misinterpretation of the "original text." If the glorious message was presented in a glad, hopeful way; let the poor sinner know that salvation is simple and easy; in fact revival meetings should be like a beautiful holiday frolic. Satan could be routed and overcome much more easily, if mild methods were used. Better use boquets than two-edged swords. Nothing can be gained by harsh terms, such as *Devil, Hell, Eternal damnation, Hell fire*, etc. The revivalist who appeals to the higher principles that are dormant in every heart, and less terrible anathemas, would be much more appreciated.

The Old Man believes that "much and lasting good" can be done if roses, honeysuckle vines, and cologne water were used more fre-

New Clothes for the Old Man. 37

quently. Many great opportunities are lost because of a misunderstanding of how to bring a Pentecost. Great care should be used in preparation; wise committees must be appointed from the membership to look after all the details of the meeting, so that the preacher and his helper can give all their time to social duties, and cultivating the good favor of everybody.

Unless the preacher or pastor takes well in the community, nothing can be done. If such a method is adopted and plenty cards distributed in the congregation the converts will be numbered by scores and hundreds. Whereas, by the old method there are sometimes no visible results at all.

The one great object to be kept in mind is to bring satisfactory things to pass. The papers will blaze abroad such tidings, the "eye of the Church" will take due cognizance of such proceedings. The Old Man has made a special study of evangelism, and has much to say about the best methods, and urges all interested parties to take due notice. What is the use of raising a big row, wounding the feelings of

Satan, offending the best people in the church, insulting the best and latest discoveries in religious thought; far better have a quiet "Confirmation service," "Decision Day" or "First Communion," than all this we hear about broken-heartedness, "praying through," etc. Since the old methods have become obsolete, we are rapidly taking the world for Christ. The Old Man says, yea and amen.

IN WHICH THE TEXTURE OF AN
OUTTER GARMENT IS EXAMINED.

CHAPTER IV

IN WHICH THE TEXTURE OF AN OUTTER GARMENT IS EXAMINED.

The third side-light which we shall mention is one of the most dangerous of all, because the most beautiful. The hideous, the ugly, the distorted can be easily avoided; we naturally shrink from anything that is labeled dangerous, but we are easy victims to the poison in the pot bubbling over with that which delights the eye and papilla. The Old Man has a strong esthetic nature; under proper environment becomes susceptible to the finest expressions of culture.

It seems incredulous that this "root of all sin and bitterness" could be so touched up as to shine in the highest circles of society, and also adorn the most fastidious parlors. In fact there is a subtle phase of the Old Man's character that prefers this to the coarse and vulgar. Why? The more of the "beautiful show" possessed, the less likelihood of ever being brought to a sense of soul poverty and contrition of heart. Repentance is impossible when there is self-congratulation; the consciousness of any power possessed that will attract, entertain, and control people, hedges up the way for the work of prevenient grace. Such natures are shocked at even being compared with the low and vile of earth. They can see and appreciate the good, the artistic, the beautiful of earth, sea, and sky, while the "common clay" lives only to enjoy the sensuous nature.

This peculiar class of the Old Man's brood of children believe in churches and religion, but that the high and low should have their own places of worship. The poor and illiterate should not be embarrassed by the presence of their superiors; likewise the "better class" should not be disturbed and mortified by the uncomely occupying the pew in front or behind. Such an arrangement would be incongruous.

Prominent among the adorable fine arts loved and worshiped by the Old Man is music. Nothing is so inspiring; nothing stirs such lofty emotions as music. That is, when it is real music; the visions and conceptions of great

New Clothes for the Old Man. 43

master souls; not the harsh jugglery of sound called music by the rifraff. Public worship should not be degraded by anything but high-grade compositions, vocal or instrumental. Both should occupy a large part of the Sunday programme. The best part of the religious service is ruined without the proper kind of music.

This splendid "drawing card" should not be sacrificed, even if suitable musicians are not available among the membership. The high-tenor who gambles on Saturday nights and Sunday afternoons should be utilized to beautify the service; the contralto who is a society belle, plays cards, dances, goes to theatres, and drinks wine should not waste her talent singing only for the worldly.

The pulpit and pew are often in perfect harmony, drinking alike at this melliferous fountain. An anthem rendered just before the sermon prepares the hearers to receive the Word gladly. There was no message in song, but just the power of music. The Old Man is very partial to the old hymns that have been set as solos and anthems, so that all the words are lost in the trills and semi-quivers of vocal gymnastics. How boresome would be "Show pity, Lord, oh Lord forgive; Let a repentant sinner live," as our fathers sang it at the altar when souls were struggling for freedom. There is no need or demand for such singing as would inflame the soul and cause it to sweep upward by mighty faith and lay hold of precious promises through the blood. Music has been revolutionized and elevated, it no longer appeals to a superstitious fancy, but to refined souls who can place a true estimate upon it.

Literature comes next in order among the fine arts. To know literature is an indispensable accomplishment. No one is so shorn of strength as he who is ignorant of these wide, fertile plains of knowledge; no preacher can bring a wholesome, living gospel who has not communed in such higher strata of thought. All that is great and good in human character has been arranged for us by master minds. If we want to feel the touch of ten-talented men we must seek for them in literature.

What can be more toothsome and attractive than a lecture on Sunday night on some great character in fiction when the congregation is

New Clothes for the Old Man. 45

made up of young men and women who need to learn some real life lessons? Or better still an analysis of some great poetic creation? The versatile preacher could find endless variety, and thereby save his ministry from the humdrum monotony so prevalent among so-called orthodox preachers.

Character sketches or studies on Emerson, Browning, Hugo, Tennyson, Wordsworth, Poe, *et al*, are always throbbing with interest. We once heard an eminent Methodist divine address a great Sunday night audience on Plato. How much better was that than to have sent the congregation away depressed and discouraged under a load of sin. We were made to feel how much good there was in heathen philosophy.

There are some very helpful lessons that might be drawn from Moses, Elijah, Daniel, John the Baptist, and Paul, and no doubt should have the preference when preaching to children, but for adults and wiser heads Hamlet, Jean Valjean, and Hypatha are more realistic.

A leading Methodist author and divine once

said in our hearing: "I was killed and made alive by reading Emerson." Shades of Mr. Wesley! This embassador of Christ had been transformed by the Unitarian sage. He had been *Emersonized;* and the Old Man said Amen.

IN WHICH THE COLOR RECEIVES
DUE ATTENTION.

CHAPTER V.

IN WHICH THE COLOR RECEIVES DUE ATTENTION.

We can not leave the subject discussed in the last chapter without mentioning another phase, which by many is considered the most beautiful trait of the Old Man's wonderful make-up. Whoever preaches that the *Fall* left only a vile and degraded nature is far from the facts in the case. He has the sparkle of a genius; he has the ability to roam in the highest strata of conceptions and imagery. What can be compared with a soul enamored and enraptured by the mysteries of color? No daubing or cheap chromo business; but oh the joy to behold the delicate blending of light and shade gathered from the valleys, the cloud-land, the storm or raging sea. All the pigment of the rain-bow transmitted to the canvas so that trees, birds, flowers, and human souls throb with animation. No greater studies than the faces of Minerva or Juno; those heathen ideals of the gods. Think how much the religion of Christ owes to sacred art. Those Madonnas, Crucifixions, and Apostolic scenes.

None but choice souls spend time in an art gallery. A preacher who is able to give a dissertation on the Masters, both mediaeval and modern—should be appointed where such sweetness could not waste on the desert air. What a wonderful gospel can be preached by those who have added to their scholarship the beautiful dreams of the artist.

Nothing cultivates proportion, form and symmetry like the *nude in art*. Some objection of course, may be raised to this special department; however, such is surely confined to fogyism of the past. Specimens of such art adorn the very best parlors and galleries, and are admired by the most fastidious. Because such masterpieces are sometimes found in saloons, billiard halls, and men's clubs, they should not be discarded from places of refinement. Like a lady who defended her low-necked dress by saying: "To the pure all things are pure." Let us therefore exhibit *Rembrandt* wherever possible and consider it a privilege.

New Clothes for the Old Man.   51

To be a student of the beautiful is soon to be a student of the good and true. We once knew a leading young Methodist preacher who was permitted to spend a year from his conference studying in Germany and Italy. No wonder he could devote ten successive nights *"With the Masters."* The bright colors of Titan, Turner, Raphael and Angelo are far better adapted to the needs of the average congregation than the crimson wave of Cavalry that washes our sins away. The Old Man will gladly sign a petition for the return of a pastor so gifted, or to remove one unable to satisfy the esthetic spirit of the saints.

It should make no difference whatever, that the most cruel, barbarous and licentious age of the church was when art was at its zenith. Many believe that modern painters have never reached such excellence as did those masters of Mediaeval art, and no age has been more licentious.

It should make no difference that those grand conceptions are but exponents of the low standards, superstitions, and ecclesiastical prostitutions of sacred truth. They please and satisfy that part of the race which loves the form of godliness but denies that there be any power. It should make no difference that religious denominations which lay greatest stress on such external representations of faith, atonement, suffering, and sainthood, are *spiritually dead* so far as salvation is concerned. Such a thing as the witness of God's Spirit to sonship and adoption is not even dreamed of, much less realized. We mean this of course from the standpoint of evangelical faith and experience. No doubt the teachers, preachers and communicants of such organizations would look with contempt and scorn at the idea that they were not the elect of heaven.

The Old Man believes that Munkacsy has made a great contribution to the religious world; that his "Christ Before Pilate" has given a living reality to that dramatic scene, and that faith has been greatly enriched by the picture of the howling mob and the silent Christ. The original has sold for a princely fortune, and those who have seen it are highly favored above their fellows and brothers.

Our readers must not understand that we

care nothing for the great productions of those master spirits; far from it. We honor them as ten talented men, and revel before their creations, and believe that no better adornment could be placed in a Christian home than *some* of those paintings, but we have never heard of the Holy Spirit using the *Sestine Madonna* or any other great painting for the salvation of a soul. The Old Man would persuade us that our esthetic taste is religion, there is such a kinship to the divine. Something must be done to take the place of a living faith, and what matters how lovely the sentiment, if the real thing is lost in the process. Anything that is to be coveted and gives satisfaction to the possessor is all the more dangerous. A Scriptural warning to "be not deceived" is timely. Artists and art lovers, like many of the most gifted musicians and music lovers, *are far away from God*. How easy to worship a "Last Judgment" on canvas and have no thought of the *Deis Ira;* to worship a "Messiah" sung by vocal experts and know nothing about "God with us" through Christ.

IN WHICH THE BEAUTY IS SEEN
AT A DISTANCE.

CHAPTER VI.

IN WHICH THE BEAUTY IS SEEN AT A DISTANCE.

The next side light we shall notice bearing upon that "seven heads and ten horns" combination is that while the Old Man antedates all organizations and endeavors, he has the genuine stamp of a modern product. Up-to-date and thoroughly imbued with the spirit of this generation. So important and so legitimate, no one shall be able to gainsay that which has brought the church and her great achievements in the public eye. It is a great mistake to suppose that the Lord's work can be carried on in a corner. Satan blazes his work abroad and thereby creates enthusiasm. Should not we go and do likewise? His motto is: Do it, and do it now; let the other fellow know that you have done it.

The Old Man is a great church worker and enjoys the reputation so justly merited. There is no place in the church militant for the drone. Not only should things be done, but a careful tabulated report should be made. The most minute details touching the *mint*, the *anise* and *cummin* should be conscientiously guarded. Statistics showing just how far the cart bearing the ark has moved. Even the axle-grease used on the sacred whels of the cart should be given due credit. There are no non-essentials when we are gleaning for the Master. Nothing talks like cold figures, and when Satan beholds a startling array of arithmetical certainties he knows that his end is near, even at the very door. A preacher of all others should bring things to pass. His authority and commission are of such magnitude, the dignity of his office takes first rank over all other dignities, recognizing, however, the superior rank of officers who are over him, lest strange fire should be found on his altar, and unsavory incense fill the temple. Independence of thought and movement must never be allowed free course. Ancient traditions should be preserved at all hazards.

A preacher should not care if some one of the baser sort call him an ecclesiastical tax-gatherer; he is a church worker and must turn his face like flint and allow no stone unturned until all the assessments are well in hand. Begin early, never stop until every dollar is in the hands of the various boards. Have bazaars, basket dinners, picnics, suppers, special meetings and entertainments. Plan ways and means for full reports. A splendid time to raise money by public collection is when the revival is at high tide; at the close of a warm sermon when every one is more or less under conviction for sin. They are in trouble and will be easily persuaded to take out a policy against *fire*. A few funny stories may be thrown in to keep up good spirits; this of course will destroy the conviction, but what of it; the subscription has been landed and mind eased for another year.

The bantam feather rightly belongs to the dear brother who gets money, builds churches, helps colleges with a swing of victory. No honors should be withheld from those who have *in the name of Jesus done many wondrous works, and prophesied in high places.* We shall examine this special department of the Old Man's views of consecrated finance later.

It is delightful indeed to have the "church worker" reputation at the time of conferences and other gatherings for the promotion of the larger interests of the church. Stewards and presidents of woman's societies gladly magnify their office during the sessions of the district and annual conferences, especially when bishops and other connectional brethren are present. The Old Man enjoys a place on the programme, or on an important committee. What is nicer than to read a paper on some great theme before an august body of clerical brethren; such zeal, such consecration, such liberality as we may then hear; such yearning after the higher things of the gospel.

The Old Man is at his best when called upon to entertain some distinguished churchman, if the rank and calibre is far up the scale. The thing is done with such grace and magnificence that the dear visiting brethren would remark (and we have heard them), "What a privilege to serve such people."

Our beneficent host and hostess have not attended prayer-meeting for months, they take no part in the Sunday-school, were never heard

New Clothes for the Old Man. 61

to testify and rarely seen at the service on Sunday night, but during the conference they pass *ad summum valorem* with all except the silent pastor who has the courtesy to keep still.

The prayer and class-meetings are regarded as work of supererogation; the regular Sunday morning service, if the worshiper be in the proper frame of mind, will furnish spiritual food sufficient for the week. There are a few unstable souls who are always praying, always being tried and sorely tempted; super-sensitive over some small imaginary sin that short rations will not satisfy; not so with our hospitable friends. Every service during the conference must be attended, if possible. Those appointed to preach on such occasions represent more than local interests. The bishop, secretary or editor has no more appreciative hearer than the subject of this sketch. The Old Man is patience and charity personified during a long-dry-get-no-where sermon; some times endures the trying ordeal of hearing a sermon from manuscript, and is the first one to rush to the preacher and tell him how much they have been helped.

The church supper furnishes a fine opportunity for the display of zeal. The chit-chat—the chink of coins—the rattle of dishes are musical. Great satisfaction is felt if "my cake" is selected to adorn the table while the others are being devoured. Mrs. Old Man's cake can be sold at auction or voted to the prettiest girl, adding much to the Lord's exchequer. To be a success at these religious(?) assemblies one must fume and sweat and scold one moment over "having everything to do," and "money that is not being turned in properly, etc., etc.," and smile the next moment on all the patrons, and laugh cheerily over church gossip. When dressed in low neck and short sleeves they serve each customer in a way that makes them feel they have gotten the worth of their money in church work with a vengeance, and the Old Man is proficient.

IN WHICH THE CASH VALUES ARE CONSIDERED.

CHAPTER VII.

IN WHICH THE CASH VALUES ARE CONSIDERED.

The Old Man takes a very keen interest in every department of church work; no one can be more thoroughly awake to the needs, emergencies, and exegencies of every local organization of God's kingdom on earth. He recognizes a spirit of lethargy, that is almost universal, which ought to be stimulated and overcome. What an opportunity the church is losing when she persists in maintaining some antiquated superstition about *sinlessness* or *dying to the world* and does not read the signs of the times. It is nothing more nor less than practicing the words of the Master when He said: "The children of this world are wiser in their generation than the children of light." The affairs of the world are in perfect harmony with the pulse of the new century. New tricks, schemes and methods are winning notoriety and fortune in the commercial world daily. No man can hope to succeed in the sharp competition who does not corner the situation somehow or somewhere. This is an administration of *frenzied finance;* the alert business man sees this and plunges in for a lion's share. Is there any law of reason or ethics to compel the church to hold aloof and be forever embarrassed and humiliated as a result? Nay, verily.

The Old Man thinks that it is a positive shame that the church, the greatest institution on earth, must be hindered and limited because of a lack of money making sense. He has devoted whole pages in leading magazines, on hints for raising money, and yet so few seem to profit by his timely suggestions.

There is not a month in the whole year but that some attraction may be boomed in a way to bring the *flocks militant* together, and be in harmony with the season. People are going to be entertained, and they are willing to spend their money for it. If the pastor, in co-operation with his official board and the "good women," is wise enough to always have something new, fresh, original and toothsome, they cannot come too often for the innocent, simple-hearted communicants. Such coming together always promotes *sociability, co-operation, familiar acquaintance, concentrated zeal, gastronomic liberality, financial economy,* and *religious pleasure.* Now if advancement in all this galaxy of good things does not promote piety and growth in grace, the Old Man is willing to acknowledge his utter inability to pass judgment on anything worth while.

Now for a practical proposition. In the latter part of January after festivities of the holidays and special evangelical services are over, an oyster supper with music by colored orchestra would make a splendid attraction. If a little time and money be spent in advertising and care be used that the food-stuffs be not too rich or highly seasoned, enough money may be cleared to pay off the Home and Foreign Mission claims in one night. The Boards are always in great need at that season, and an early remittance is always appreciated.

February would be a good time for a new feature: say a *Boston Bean Party* with comic literary adjuncts. Then something about Easter to suit, and, as the season advances, strawberries, ice-cream, crazy quilt bazaars, lawn fetes, Gypsy Camps, foot shows, etc. It might be well to explain the last mentioned. When the supper or refreshments are ready, the ladies retire behind a curtain, remove their shoes and stockings (weather being warm), then the brethren can select their partners from the *pedal exhibit*, the curtain being raised a few inches. Any man who is loyal and loves the church would gladly pay $1.00 for such wholesome privileges.

The entire cycle of months may be made in this manner, until the *menu* gets back to pumpkin pies and oysters. The little petty quarrels growing out of such a grand circle of good things and good times are not worthy to be compared with the financial saving realized. The money accumulated from good crops, good business, good speculations, and good wages may flow out in channels of luxury, culture, adornment, or travel. Very little of it need be used to help a Cause that owns all the wealth, namely, gold, silver, and the cattle on a thousand hills.

Several families will not speak for months

and years, but if they are careful to sit in opposite sides of the church no special harm will come. The pastor who is unable to come up to the help of the sisters, to the help of the sisters against the big financial burdens, will find rough sailing, and ought to. He should be ready at the call of the Pastor's Aid Society to lay off his coat, collar and cravat and fix tables, stoves, turn the ice-cream freezer, or solicit hams and cakes from the congregation. By the sweat of our brow we must serve our day and generation. Woe be to the man who emphasizes his call to *preach* and does not propose to *hew wood and draw water*. Such a pastor deserves financial shortage for himself and humiliation before the conference, because the collections are *not* all in full.

The Old Man cannot understand why so much noise and grumbling should be made over the fact that Sister A. "has all the work to do"; Sister B. promised to be present to help wait on the table, and never came until everyone had eaten; Sister C. lost most of her spoons, which were given as a wedding present, although she tied red strings around the handles; Sister D.

should have had some one else with her to receive the money; there was a tremendous leakage somehow. Sister E. promised to furnish her colored girl, two chickens and four pies, and failed to do it; that the young women prefer to have a good time talking to the boys rather than serve tables.

All such friction confuses the *patron saint* of the modern festival, but some will move away, others will die, some families will intermarry, and in a few years the waters of Zion will be quiet. The Old Man is always optimistic, and cannot bear a pessimistic view of any situation.

IN WHICH THE SIZE OF GARMENTS IS STUDIED.

CHAPTER VIII.

IN WHICH THE SIZE OF GARMENTS IS STUDIED.

Another phase of modern church life that finds an earnest response to our venerable companion, viz.: the love of big demonstrations, such as conventions, conferences, assemblies, etc. He believes that nothing promotes religious life like the enthusiasm of such gatherings. If it happens to be a young people's society in annual, national assembly, every one should be urged to attend. The traveling expenses of crossing the state or nation is quite an item, but they see so much, and will be so much more religious after it is over. Think of ten thousand young men and women seated in a great tabernacle catching a word now and then from the paper being read by Dr. Skylight of Star Valley on the "Philosophy of Soul Introspection." The pastor who does not urge his Epworth League to attend at any cost, can not expect them to grow in grace. When a meeting of this character is held in a city Satan fairly holds his breath. Don't he see the bunting and banners flying, and everybody wearing badges and state pins to show where they are from? Don't he hear the shouting, singing and speeches being made by various delegations desiring to raid his kingdom by taking the meeting to their place the next time? The whole city is taken by storm; night comes on, the multitudes that have rushed from one attraction to another retire with body and brain at the point of exhaustion; but they are in the swing, attending the greatest thing in the land at the call of the church, and certainly becoming deeply spiritual as a result. Besides the bulwarks of sin will scarcely recover to normal operation when the convention closes, and the strongholds of Satan throughout the land will surely be affected by the great spiritual force generated at that ocean, mountain, or lake city.

Did not Moses establish these great feasts, we are in prophetic and patriarchal succession, who can deny it. No greater privilege than to sit for a month with the highest law making body of a church; it is the *summum bonum*. One great denomination expended almost a quarter of a million in such a conference. This included banquets, excursions, concerts and special entertainments; but during the month many men were elected to high places; great speeches were made over the distinctions of law and ritual, creed terminology, etc.; thus be it far from any one to say that the money was not wisely spent. The Old Man is thoroughly convinced from past experience that no greater means of grace has yet been hit upon, than one-dollar-a-plate banquets for our young people. The toast-master should be selected on the reputation of piety, and all the responses given by those who are qualified to make a hit with eloquence or funny stories.

There is no department of religious life in which the Old Man has more decided views than the revival question. Lucky is the preacher who feels a call into a wider evangelism. When once his name gets into the papers, and a market is created for his goods in church commercialism, there is no limit to his usefulness. Men of extraordinary ability can hold a union meeting; get a gifted singer to accompany and organize the chorus; hold the services in the town hall or theater; scatter bills, bring things to pass. The whole town gets interested; the news gets into metropolitan papers; wealthy men get warmed up and a great collection of cash is insured. The evangelist soon discovers himself to be no ordinary man, and his remuneration for a two or three weeks' meeting should be equal to the pay of a pastor for a whole year. All this can be done with two dozen sermons, touched up with incidents and illustrations. Cards can be signed by the converts and it is so easy to number them in the hundreds; then a score of other cities will pull for a similar meeting. Three such meetings were held: Conversions reported as follows: three-four and six hundred, respectively. Amounts paid evangelists were five, seven and eleven hundred dollars. The small town where six hundred were saved (?) voted for whisky two months after. Where the three and four hundred were saved(?) in towns of less than two thousand, not one real case of salvation could be found two months after, and the prayer meetings, poorly attended, were without praise or victory.

New Clothes for the Old Man. 77

When the people of Methodist training and tradition feel that there must be revival services, the kind mentioned is preferable above all others. On general principles the Old Man would do away with the revival and substitute "confirmation," "first communion," or "decision day." It is so beautiful to have the children lined up, the girls dressed in white with long veils, white slippers, and covered with flowers. The ceremony is so impressive and no child will ever forget that day or how they were dressed.

The old antiquated, slaughter-house theory of the *Blood* is no longer adapted to the needs of children who have grown up in the Sunday school and church.

The Old Man pities the preacher who labors under the delusion that men, women and children must separately and individually, seek a personal Savior, by deep heart sore repentance and faith. Church work should be done on a broad scale. The old mourners' bench method did not save the world, and the new method does. The world is rapidly being brought to Christ; the powers of darkness are being overthrown by the new plan of salvation. Suffer a timely exhortation from the Old Gentleman of the new school—get busy, travel, make speeches, meet with conferences and boards; if a revival is wanted appoint conservative, discreet committees to look after the thing on business principles; get up a "Forward Movement," pull for college endowments; cultivate men of wealth. Leave the business of getting men saved to those who are incapable of doing greater things. Get busy—the Master's business requires haste. Be a worker that despises small things.

IN WHICH PRACTICAL STYLES ARE RECOMMENDED.

CHAPTER IX

IN WHICH PRACTICAL STYLES ARE RECOMMENDED.

We shall now consider what may be verbosely termed "practical common sense religion." That which deals with the concrete and not the abstract; with the tangible and not the intangibles; with the real and not the unreal. The Old Man makes a railing indictment against the church for dealing so much with the vague and unseen.

What the world needs today is not a theological creed, faith, prayers, fasting, consecration, etc., but a stalwart, robust type of dealing with humanity as we find it. There was a time when men went to war over the meaning of a word, contended for the number of angels that could dance on the point of a needle; but we no longer roam in such quagmires. What is the difference if some able and well informed men do not believe in the Incarnation, authenticity of the Bible, the certainty of a hell, or the personality of the Holy Ghost. A man's usefulness cannot be measured by such technicalities. The opposition to such men, because of these things, is harsh and unbrotherly. Let men believe whatever they wish, and preach whatever they wish. It is doing things that counts. The "Good Samaritan" is the ideal. Help the unfortunate; alleviate physical suffering rather than waste time and money trying to accomplish what the bigot calls "conversion." The man who is a victim of strong drink, abuses his wife and children, squanders his money, or lives in a hut on some island where clothes have not yet been introduced needs anything worse than some imaginary hypnotic transformation, the shiboleth of orthodoxy. Physical need is the first law of nature. Get them food, clothes, employment; build hospitals, libraries, schools. All these things make civilization, and not creeds and theologies.

The Old Man believes that carrying a so-called gospel to the "regions beyond," is as impracticable as the conversions as reported from those regions. The "Heathen at home" should claim our first attention. They need our help.

New Clothes for the Old Man. 83

Why send so much money away, when there is such misery and suffering at home. "Who knows what becomes of the money sent away off yonder?" The command to go into the world, the slogan of missionary cranks, is undoubtedly spurious, like many oft-quoted passages.

It is very interesting to notice the quick descent in temperature of the Old Man's zeal and practicability, when a claim is presented for the Heathen at Home. At once you can hear of the most appalling calamities, such as floods, hot winds, droughts, sickness, and hard times, generally. The wolf at once puts in appearance, and the interest which is manifested in those loved ones whom God has called him to care for, becomes tender and pathetic. He will almost weep over the great needs of our *home heathen*, and declare how much joy it would give to be able to just support the whole movement alone. Who has not heard such remarks as: "If I had as much money as some people, etc., etc."

It sometimes requires a Holy Ghost dissecting knife and a gospel microscope to discover the Old Gentleman under so much make-believe righteousness; but he is there full grown and matured. No better place to get a life-size view, than when an effort is being made to raise money for the preacher or evangelist, under whose ministry he has laughed, wept and shouted. Nothing is so distasteful as *money matters;* he at once gets interested in the salvation of some soul who will not hear the gospel because the time is taken up trying to get filthy lucre. The service has been spoiled when good might have been done. There was a time when we could attend worship without hearing money all the time. The cloven hoof is there.

But, we must not think for a moment that our time honored hero of a thousand battles is forever narrow, stingy, or short-sighted. If he has one characteristic or accomplishment above another it is that he can be adjusted to suit the occasion. He is equal to any emergency.

Remember his practical humanitarian principles. If public opinion and popular sentiment are drifting toward liberal views and apparent unselfishness, no one can excel the Old Man. The subscription list will be headed by an

New Clothes for the Old Man. 85

amount that will astonish the other interested parties. We once saw $1,000 subscribed by a man after being allowed to come before eight thousand people and tell them how much he believed in the Bible. It was a loud proclamation; if trumpets had been there they would have been flourished. "Behold here was a great man, a rich man, a mighty influence, breeder of race horses, standing before this great audience telling them that he believed that there was a God, and that he had never doubted it for one moment."

The Old Man never turns down an opportunity to do a great, noble, magnanimous deed, where the influence can be felt throughout the land. Mr. Wesley said that it would be a sad day for the church when rich men were indispensable. Such a sentiment is an injustice to our noble laymen; the great work now in hand must have access to this consecrated wealth, and full acknowledgement should be made in the columns of our church papers. "Gen. A. has given $5,000 for the work in—; Judge B. has given $1,000 for endowment, etc." The Old Man is for Foreign Missions, Home Missions, or no missions at all; for colleges or no colleges, as the case may be; he is pro or con, anti, anti-anti anything, everything or nothing. Whatever is done, however, must be practical common sense, and no foolishness.

IN WHICH CLEANING AND PRESSING IS URGED.

CHAPTER X

IN WHICH CLEANING AND PRESSING IS URGED.

No part of the old man's character commands greater applause or brings a higher price on the world market than good behavior and gentle manners. It means something to have it said of a man: "He is a gentleman." Every door opens with a spring to such an one. Clubs, lodges and churches all alike understand the value of such a catch.

The Old Man is a judge of such matters and the soul is course-grained indeed that does not study with a conscience all the niceties of speech-accent, and repertoire for all occasions. Few ever become proficient in proper decorum. People who imagine they have some great mission in the world or some noble purpose in life, will never spend a sufficient amount of time on themselves to become a real gentleman of the first waters. It is the bright, hopeful, happy soul that sees rainbows everywhere, that becomes an adept in *niceness*.

The pulpit, of all places, should be adorned by one who can arouse the latent sparks of good by gentleness and sympathy with everything and everybody. A loud, fire-baptized sermon against that visionary, hazy subject called *sin*, is very offensive, and sometimes shocking. The waves of conviction stirred up in the souls of a congregation is simply ridiculous. It is very amusing to the Old Man to hear a Bar-jonas thundering away on some terrible theme, and at the same time use grammar in a way as to grate on the finer sensibilities. A preacher should never allow his vocabulary to include harsh words; his messages should be couched in terms that suggest only love and tenderness. A preacher of the gospel who fails to study all the social demands of his congregation and all classes, is making a very grave mistake. A good stock of old stories and jokes should be kept "on tap"; and if they can be revamped in such a way as to lend freshness and apparent originality, all the better. Nothing guarantees a good hearing on the Sabbath like the preacher who is ever surrounded on week-days by a crowd of men, composed of professionals, mer-

New Clothes for the Old Man. 91

chants, street gentlemen, and idle loafers, laughing at the witticisms that spontaneously burst from his sacred lips. "That is my kind of a preacher," may be heard from every source. Just think of the low and vile conversations that are smothered out because of the parson's presence. Such an influence is far reaching.

The great outside, sinful classes will gladly hear the gospel from the minister who can apply this great endowment to advantage. The Old Man never enjoys seeing any one, especially a preacher, take life too seriously. The gloom of guilty conscience hangs entirely too much over the multitudes; the better way is not to pile it on thicker but to make every circle happy by fresh puns and conundrums. Life has too many shadows, why not help them to forget their troubles and even their sins. "Let bygones be by-gones"; "don't grieve over spilt milk." To do so is poor policy.

The preacher who expects to reach the largest circle of people, must never appear to be burdened; such a mood has a depressing influence and is of course a very poor advertisement for his religion of cheer.

A great book has been written in this country entitled "Skilled Labor for the Master"; it is full of timely helps and suggestions, but the Old Man would have another chapter written by all means, viz.: study to be a shining social success; fully qualified to mingle freely in the wealthiest homes of the city. No uneasiness will ever be felt for the success of such a pastor.

The above characteristics, so necessary to the success of Christian workers, are not confined to the ministry but should predominate with all men and women who hope to be leaders in Zion.

Another important item must not be overlooked. The Old Man is a specialist on sickroom etiquette, if the sufferer happens to belong to the same social rank of himself—or still more proficient if they grade a few notches higher. The sick room will be brightened at once by floral tokens or delicacies of the season, with accompanying note: "Lovingly," or "For your speedy recovery" and many other touching remembrances. There may have existed before no special attachment for the sick one or there may have been envy or jealousy, but out of tenderness of the Old Man's heart comes the expression of love and forgiveness. The Old Man believes in reciprocity; the flowers, notes and oranges will be remembered and doubly returned at the first opportunity. If you want to see the subject of our sketch tower up in might and beauty, wait until a funeral occurs. The pastor's wife or the president of the woman's missionary society can not reach the scene of sorrow before "Mrs. So and So." Such kindness and sympathy. The multitude of friends and neighbors will be given an object lesson of how deeply Mr. and Mrs. Old Man have felt for the bereaved family when the flowers are put on exhibition. The largest and most expensive design will stand up before all, "With Sympathy."

Dear readers, do not think for one moment that all such things as we have just mentioned, may not be done in Jesus' name; but too often He is not thought of and the sickly sentimentality perishes with the using, or is consumed in its own pride and self-flattery.

IN WHICH THE CLOTHING IS UP-TO-DATE FOR PLACE AND SEASON.

CHAPTER XI

IN WHICH THE CLOTHING IS UP-TO-DATE FOR PLACE AND SEASON.

The next side-light which the lantern-slide of close observation reveals, is a very distinctive one; in it the Old Man scarcely hides his identity. But even here there is a wide-spread approbation, and the unwary followers are legion. In no way is the Old Man so up-to-date as on the question of modern worldliness. He heartily approves the modern idea *in toto*. Why put oneself against the godly opinions and judgments of some of the ablest pillars, both in the clergy and laity? To the Old Man the term *worldliness* is a misnomer; what the fanatics harp over is but the legitimate expression of our innocent natures. To deny our people, especially the young, the enjoyment of social diversions is to lay burdens on them too grievous to bear. Such standards transcend the very latest interpretation of Christian principles. James 4:4, along with many other passages, is known to be spurious. What can be more ridiculous than to say that whoever lives in such a way as to be true to himself as he finds himself, is an "*enemy to God.*"..Booh! Away with such superanuated straight-jacketness!

God has given us our natures and He has given us the world in which to enjoy them. The Old Man is not so unreasonable as to charge the Creator with such inconsistency as to endow us with desires, propensities and appetites that are not to be gratified. No doubt by these cruel and impossible demands the church militant is losing heavily each year and failing to add recruits that would have joined in the holy warfare but for the extreme and impractical position assumed. "Wisdom is always justified of her children."

But a brighter day is dawning for the church; We should be profoundly thankful that she is at last getting away from her puritanic narrowness. Our people can be faithful communicants and yet enjoy life, and it is the rankest mossbackism to deny them such a privilege. The preacher who so far misused his power as to enforce the whole letter and spirit of church law, demanding of all, rich and poor, great and small alike, that they cease to travel on Sunday trains, buy groceries, go to the post-office on the Sabbath; attend theaters, card parties, shows, dances, wine drinking and the like, will certainly bring down upon his head the wrath not only of the ablest supporters of the church, but in some localities the *powers that be*. The Old Man believes that such a policy would be unwise in the extreme. To preach boldly and continuously against such things would result in shortness of congregation, accessions, finances, and in fact the church would surely suffer in every department.

Our venerable ally really enjoys a breezy report of what has been done, and a policy that cuts out things to be reported is nothing less than a calamity. For a good man to lose out simply because he has failed to weigh all the *mint, anise* and *cummin* is very unjust.

Then what is the use; what can be done? The answer is obvious; nothing; people are going to follow their natural tendencies, and why drive them away by erratic methods? We should not break a bruised reed, but in much charity love them back to where they will not spend nearly so much time and money on what seemeth to profit but little.

We must not overlook one very significant point on the question of worldly amusement; the Old Man most heartily believes that promiscuous dancing at questionable places, and attending vile, licentious plays should be discouraged, and he thinks that such diversions should be spoken against in no uncertain language. No good can come from the vaudeville and the coarse *can-can*; only the best should be patronized, and if preachers and cultured people would lead in those matters by precept and example, no doubt a great reform would soon come. Wise discrimination is very necessary; some balls at certain places should be discountenanced, especially during any of the holy seasons. We must not so forget ourselves as to seek pleasure at such times as the church, with her time-honored traditions, says we should give ourselves to various abstinences and fastings.

No sensible Christian man could afford to miss a great international exhibit like a World's Fair. Only the back numbered, out of date brethren even suggest such a thing. The whole world is brought to our doors, and the over-conscientious who do not believe in small shows should approve *the greatest show on earth.* Preachers who expect to occupy places of honor are too wise to miss such a world wide sweep of knowledge.

The Old Man has no sympathy whatever with the war that is being waged in some sections against lodges; these great beneficent orders that are banded together for the upbuilding of the race. They do as much good as the church. Many people prefer the lodges because of the beautiful symbols and high moral teachings. The truth is that after all the man who lives up to the standard of many of the lodges, will have a religion superior to many church members. "He that is not against us is for us"—and every one knows that lodges have no special objection even to the deeper works of grace. If we follow the standard set up by the Old Man we will surely be received into an *Eternal habitation.*

IN WHICH VIEWS OF A PARTICU-
LAR STYLE ARE FREELY
EXPRESSED.

CHAPTER XII.

IN WHICH VIEWS OF A PARTICULAR STYLE ARE FREELY EXPRESSED.

The last side-light which we shall endeavor to throw on the Old Man's character is one that has done much to win for him the commendation and approbation of this generation. The thought almost dazes one, but a moment of sober reflection will remove all the mystery. The Old man believes in *entire sanctification*. Not only so, but he has decided views, terminologies, information, authorities to sustain his position. How could anyone read the Bible and not believe this doctrine; but with much show of profundity, declares: "I don't believe in some men's theories." His is a common-sense, practical, flesh and blood, success in business, political party sort of sanctification; the only kind that can be promulgated with any degree of satisfaction to the present day congregation. It is a great mistake, in fact it is rashness not to accept the statement of doctrine handed down to us who are of limited calibre, by the universities, especially if such faculties received their finishing touches at German institutions of learning. These are great schools, and scholars have looked into the *rationale* of all such questions; and for a person, whose only source of light and information has been a few hours wrestling in the straw, to question such authority is presumption and bigotry gone to seed. Many of the learned doctors and retired prophets have pronounced the theology of higher thought entirely sound.

It does not matter at all that those great theologians differ among themselves; each has a beautiful statement of the truth. The "Zinzindorfian" and "growth" theory are in no way antagonistic to each other. Each one is entirely Biblical and satisfactory. Both reach the same results, should there be any discord. Sensible sanctification is always characterized by its harmonious and unifying powers. No church was ever divided when either of these theories was faithfully preached. There is such an at-one-ment about them that no controversy is ever provoked. Ecclesiastical authority never interferes with personal rights if properly exercised.

It is also noteworthy that those who are sanctified at conversion or by growth are far too humble to testify or make any noise about it. The Old Man is very conscientious and prefers to have his "light shine" rather than blow a trumpet to be seen of men. The line by line, precept by precept, a little here and a little there is so much more preferable than a ringing testimony that the Blood cleanses from all sin by faith. It smacks with bigotry and Phariseeism which are divisive and positively harmful to the more cultured congregations. Such wild statements can be allowed back in the brush where people have no better light, but entirely out of order in a church that has had the able ministry of college and seminary trained men. The Old Man is very charitable in that he believes such people and preachers to be sincere; no one should be blamed because unable to give a clear statement of a religious concept. The mistake is made in trying to palm off vague emotionalism upon people who have been long training in assimilating philosophical truth. This

"Blood Cleansing Gospel" has little or nothing in it about the poets, and the great live questions of the day.

John Wesley, Adam Clark, Fletcher, Watson, Benson, et al, all preached and taught that sanctification was a second definite work of grace wrought instantaneously by faith, subsequent to regeneration, but our later theologians have discovered that these standards are wrong. This wonderful galaxy of Holy Ghost men were good and sincere, but crooked in their theology. There is no objection or harm in having all the young preachers study and subscribe to this special Methodist doctrine and even have them promise "to groan after it," so long as it is surpressed in the pulpit and not allowed to become offensive. The doctrine seems to be Biblical and certainly Methodistic, but not workable in the face of present day ideas and tendencies.

Young preachers may believe anything they desire about our doctrines, but should be restrained from attending camp-meetings where people believe that the experience is obtainable and in every way practical. The effect of such

New Clothes for the Old Man. 109

meetings is usually lasting and incapacitates preachers and people for many modern demands of church life.

The Old Man believes in leniency and charity for the dancing, card-playing, theatre-going sister, the whiskey-defiled politician steward, the "bucket-shop" colonel trustee, the officious sister who reads papers at conferences about the *slums* and *heathen*, and at the same time wearing more jewelry than she has given for these causes in years.

But when the local preacher evangelist enters another man's preserves without permission, preaching full salvation by faith in the Blood, the administration of discipline should be speedily applied. Failure to preach our doctrines, and failing wilfully and continuously to live up to our General Rules are nothing to compare with such a breach of law as bringing salvation to scores of souls on another man's territory.

The Old Man never fails to offer some very wise, conservative advice to the individual who is seeking the blessing. He will agree with the hungry soul that he ought to have it, but great care must be exercised, as a mistake at such a time would be ruinous. Better wait days, months, or even years for the blessed experience than to get a wrong statement of the truth. If our experience tallies with the excathedra opinions of the schools, we shall be standing on a foundation that we can easily defend upon world-wide authority.

Dear reader, our subject is inexhaustible, but if we have in any way helped you to see the trail of this ancient heir of the bottomless Pit through our ramifications, we are rewarded an hundred fold. If you do not know the blessed consciousness of freedom from this "body of death," plunge into the fountain. There is power in the blood.

A PEN SKETCH WITH A WARNING

A PEN SKETCH WITH A WARNING

The stately Methodist Church on St. James boulevard, with its beautiful tower, dark granite walls, and white marble trimmings was the center of excitement and enthusiasm. It was Tuesday evening and the Home mission society was holding its regular monthly meeting. The society numbered about fifty members, being the banner auxiliary in the conference. It had been announced that matters of importance were to be discussed and a very unusual thing had happened—nearly all the members were present.

Mrs. Col. Truax, whose husband was the chairman of the official board, and by far the wealthiest man in the congregation, was the president and presided with great dignity. No doubt many had come out to hear the news. The evening papers on Monday had stated that the conference appointments would not be made before Tuesday morning. Nothing can equal the stir of a great city congregation when a new pastor is soon to come to them. Dr. Patterson, the former pastor had asked for a transfer on account of his wife's health, and the entire membership had been much exercised for weeks. Secret committees had been sent to distant cities, letters had been written to a number of bishops, and the wires had been in working order for some time, but no selection had been made, as that particular church was known to be one of the most difficult in the connection to fill.

Early Tuesday morning the appointments had been given to the *Associated Press*, but the bishop, anxious to show Col. Truax, his old friend, special favor, had wired him about the same time; but the telegram had been missent. All day the Colonel's office had been thronged with anxious enquirers, but the important yellow envelop was not delivered until the middle of the afternoon. It read as follows:

Lookout City, Sep. 15, 1905.

Col. Jereboam Truax,

Bon Ton City.

My Beloved Brother: Dr. Christopher Broadhead, a transfer from Beersheba conference is your pastor. Allow me to congratulate you and the dear people of Boulevard Church.

Your Brother,

A. M. EPISCOPOS.

On receipt of the telegram, the Colonel took a street car and hurried to the church, knowing

New Clothes for the Old Man. 115

that a large company of women would be gathered in the parlors. The chatter and babble of voices were at high tide when the Colonel's presence was announced; every one knew that he brought news concerning the much discussed subject. The far-famed doctor's name had scarcely passed the Colonel's lips before the room fairly shook with applause and congratulations. "We are fortunate," said the Colonel, "beyond our expectations."

The two weeks following this meeting were climactric, history making for that great church. Painters, paper-hangers, and carpet men, were as busy as bees around the parsonage. By the time Dr. Broadhead and his family arrived the three-story brick on the boulevard, was made new and shiny inside and out.

The two weeks following the arrival of the new pastor were a continuous round of dinings, banquets, and receptions. The Masonic lodge, the Knights Templars, the Commercial club, the Business Mens' Smoking club, and the other pastors and denominations vied with his own church in loading down the dear doctor with glory.

A few days after conference, Col. Truax received a letter from Dr. Lex, the P. E.,

which contributed very materially to the enthusiasm caused by the bishops telegram.
It ran as follows:

"My Dear Colonel: No doubt you thought that I was apparently indifferent to your anxious appeals and inquiries concerning a suitable man for Boulevard Church. This seeming indifference was caused by my own anxiety and deep concern. To secure a pastor for that important church has given me sleepless nights. Throughout the church, I knew of but two men that, in my judgment, were capable of succeeding Dr. Patterson. One of these was under no circumstance available; the other was Dr. Broadhead, your beloved pastor. To secure him, one serious difficulty was in the way. Some months ago Dr. Broadhead, at the earnest solicitation of relatives attended a campmeeting which was held near where he was spending his vacation. This camp was one of those "Second Blessing" meetings, or as they called it the Wesleyan doctrine of Entire Sanctification; a doctrine as you know, long since obsolete in our church; and a doctrine shown to have been unbiblical by the dean of our theological department of the university and the leading scholars of our church. We understand it to have grown out

New Clothes for the Old Man. 117

of Mr. Wesley's deep piety and zeal—an error of head and not heart; besides every student of church history knows that Mr. Wesley gave it up long before he died as unsound and fanatical. Dr. Broadhead being of a strong, nervous temperment and deeply pious, was captured by a sermon preached by one of their strongest evangelists. They say that he went to the altar at every service for three days; finally professed the experience, testified and preached it with great fervor in his own church. His brethren trembled for him and but for the fact that the conference was near, which ended his pastorate there, he would have divided and ruined one of the best charges in that great conference. When you thought me silent, I was pondering these serious problems. There was much concern throughout his conference; many had grave apprehensions for his mental balance. You know it would have been a calamity for him to have come to your church holding such impracticable views. He was a subject of much prayer, and several committees of the ablest preachers of other denominations labored with him. We were over-joyed when at last he was made to see the error of his way; nothing was plainer than that he would have been ruined for further service among us. He soon saw his mistake, after the influence of those people who made such capital out of his profession, had worn off. You have no idea the letters and telegrams that have been sent. Thank goodness, we have saved him, and I feel that the entire church is to be congratulated as well as the dear people, so fortunate as to have him for their pastor. I am sure you will excuse this long letter, as it lay very close to my heart, and I am sure you are interested and glad to know all the facts. Some advocate of that doctrine might drop in and embarrass Dr. Broadhead and your people. This letter will explain matters and also fortify you. Now in the name of our beloved Church, let us thank God and go forward. Yours in much love,

A. CARDINAL LEX.

This refreshing news never got beyond the circle of the Colonel's family and a few intimate friends who were known to be in hearty sympathy with it. "It will never do," said the Colonel to a prominent member of the board and his wife, who were spending an evening there, "for those people who hold that prayer-meeting on Thursday night at old Sister Youtsey's home to ever find out that Dr. Broadhead was ever tainted with that dangerous heresy—I am sorry to say some of them are members of our church. We are under lasting obligations to dear Dr. Patterson for the way he subdued and counteracted their influence in our congregation."

"You are quite right, Colonel," said Mrs. Hightower, interrupting her husband who was also about to express his approval, "if those people should ever find out about our pastor's unfortunate experience, they would brand him as a backslider, and malign him in every possible way. To me they are impudent and disgusting. They make claims that an arch-angel could not sustain."

"They certainly have given us no little trouble," said Mrs. Truax, "Sister Youtsey and her following are opposed to all our festivals and bazaars; they even objected to the Chrysanthemum Show for the benefit of our church. For goodness sake, let us keep still."

"I think," said Mr. Hightower, "that after his sermon Sunday morning, they will never suspect him as an advocate of their fanatical notions."

"His sermon was certainly a masterful effort, and had the right ring," replied the Colonel.

Six months had passed since the evening recorded in the home of Col Truax. The new pastor had grown in popularity with the entire city as well as his own people. His Sunday night lectures on present day topics and literature had drawn great crowds. They showed the Doctor to be a great speaker, a scholar, and fully abreast with all the live questions of the day. It was Easter morning. The chimes in the tower had just ceased playing *Coronation;* the great pipe organ was beginning the prelude in a soft minor key. The splendid musical programme had drawn a great congregation; even the gallery was well filled. The floral decorations were elaborate, the altar and pulpit was a solid bank of palms, easter lillies, and orchids—besides some large vases filled with cut flowers. The entire auditorium was saturated with the perfume. Promptly at 11 o'clock the pastor entered the pulpit from the study, but after taking his seat was entirely obscured from the congregation, except those in the gallery.

The organist was beginning to sweep the keys and great waves of soul stirring vibrations were penetrating the building like peals of thunder. The voluntary was *Resurrexit* composed by one of the masters. Those in the choir, who were near enough to the pastor,

New Clothes for the Old Man. 121

noticed that he was unusually pale and showed intense nervousness. The great audience on the lower floor noticed a very excited commotion in the pulpit and choir platform; notwithstanding the same was almost obscured by the tall palms and ferns. Those in the gallery could easily see the cause and every one leaned forward with blanched faces and nervous emotion.

It was all unknown to the organist, and the music was one moment dashing away rippling and warbling like a sky lark, then in soft low notes of a night bird. The leader of the choir peered around the beautiful foliage and beckoned Col. Truax, who was in his pew enjoying the musical treat. The chorister also motioned for Dr. Brownell whose pew was near the Colonel's. By this time the entire congregation was aware of something wrong. The frightened choir girls began to scatter, the organ was hushed. Dr. Broadhead had fainted, and fallen out of his chair! He was borne to the study by the doctor and others. The congregation sat dumbfounded. Why should there have been such alarm over what might have been caused by a dozen different reasons and yet without serious results. The pastor's family pressed into the study, his children were crying and the wife deathly pale. In a moment Col. Truax came from the study and announced that the services would not be continued as the pastor had been taken suddenly ill. If that congregation had been suddenly called into the presence of the Judge eternal they would not have been more terror stricken. They began to move slowly out, but many seemed to be too much awe-struck to move. Glances were exchanged, subdued whisperings and weeping could be seen on every hand. Something had happened! A strange uneasiness seemed to take possession of all. The fashionable society woman, the sordid financier, the sport, the wicked politician, the scatter-brain clerk, the novel-reading, theater-going girl, all seemed to understand that something had happened. The news spread throughout the city like the seismic waves of earthquake. A reporter from every daily paper hurried to the parsonage, whither the sick man had been taken in a private ambulance.

To the hundreds of inquiries, doctor Brownell gave no satisfactory information, except that Dr. Broadhead was a very sick man. Two physicians and a trained nurse fought the mighty forces of disease hour after hour;

New Clothes for the Old Man. 123

life seemed to be fluttering away in spite of science, skill, lotions, and balsams. It was a desperate battle with advancing and retreating on both sides; through it all the sick man remained unconscious.

The pulpit of Boulevard Church was to be occupied that evening by Dr. Lex, the P. E., who arrived in the city very late as his train was several hours behind. No one met him at the depot, as the pastor had always attended to that, in fact, no one had thought of the night service or the presiding elder. This unusual reception disconserted the doctor somewhat, but he took a car and went at once to the parsonage on St. James Boulevard. It was almost time for the night service, and the preacher was still more astonished to find, as he passed the church, that the building was dark and unopened. He walked rapidly past with a feeling of wounded pride—he the presiding elder to occupy the pulpit of that great church and no arrangements in sight. He expected to see the crowds flocking to that one center.

A still greater shock awaited his arrival at the parsonage. A few moments before the P. E. rang the door bell, Dr. Broadhead opened his eyes, and the anxious watchers gave a sigh of relief. He gave one distressed look about the room, glaring like a frightened animal. "Is Dr. Lex here?" he said, in a choking voice. They told him that he had not arrived. Closing his eyes and grasping the hand of his wife, he uttered a deep groan. "Is there anything you want, dear?" said his wife nestling close to his face with tear-stained eyes. He made no answer, but shook his head slowly.

At this moment the servant announced the arrival of Dr. Lex, whereupon the sick man with much strength of voice asked that he be brought in at once. The two divines grasped each other's hands; before entering, however, the presiding elder had met Dr. Brownell in the hall, who was just leaving and gave him a partial report of the sad occurrence of the morning. This prepared the way for the long preamble of tender words and regrets from him when he reached the bed side. The sick man fixed his eyes steadily on those of the elder, and after a long silence said with much feeling: "Dr. Lex, you are looking at a dying man; this is my last day on earth. Since eleven o'clock, I have been in the region of the damned. I tell you that the hell which scholars and some preachers have laughed out of existence is real. I am a *lost* man!"

New Clothes for the Old Man. 125

Here the gracious elder tried to interrupt him, and the distracted family tried to interfere and comfort, but he waved them aside. "I am beyond the reach of prayers. I am *lost!* You must hear me, Doctor. It has been you and others in high ecclesiastical circles that have caused me to sell my birth-right for a mess of pottage. I have sinned against light. My doom you will find in the sixth chapter of Hebrews. No—don't pray—it is too late. By entire consecration and faith God gave me an experience so deep, so wonderful, so glorious that there was no chance for doubt. I knew what I was seeking and God gave it to me. My doom is sealed; I was trifling with God's truth, truth I was sworn to proclaim. I desire that you tell my godless, unsaved congregation just what I am telling you. They have complimented and flattered my Christless gospel, and I stultified my conscience and bartered away my soul to please them and be popular. Hush—please," he said to his weeping family, "all feeling and sorrow has gone from me, I am forced to leave this dying testimony. You must preach my funeral, and take for your text: 'In hell he lifted up his eyes.' Dr. Lex, our gospel says without holiness no man shall see God. I have no one to blame but myself. When I agreed to deny that God sanctified my soul instantaneously, by faith in the Blood—the Holy Ghost was insulted and left me forever. I warn you, my fate will be yours unless you repent and go before this great district and declare the whole truth, and warn the hell-bound devotees of worldliness and lust, to flee from the wrath to come. I have preached truth, but have not preached the whole truth. I have feared men rather than God, and to-day surrounded by all that this world can give, I have had a foretaste of my eternal shipwreck."

The elder would have fled from the room, but the poor man held on to his hand with a death grip. Every word spoken grew more fierce and raspy. He was almost shrieking at the close, "I am lost, *lost*, LOST!" Then he gave one terrible, heart-rending wail, made a desperate effort as if to sit up, a shiver went all over his frame, and he sank on the pillow without another struggle. His soul was gone into the presence of God and to meet whatever record he had made. As we have no words to depict the scenes that followed, we shall draw a veil over the winding sheet of this man once called to be a prophet of Jehovah.

Let us now glance at another scene two

New Clothes for the Old Man. 127

days later. The city press had given much space to the untimely death of a great man. "A Prince Has Fallen," so the headlines read. Letters and telegrams poured in from all over the country. The chimes at the hour above mentioned were calling the people to the funeral service of Dr. Broadhead. A long line of carriages were waiting, the largest flower wagon was insufficient to carry the cut-flower designs. The space occupied on Sunday by resurrection reminders, was now covered by death tokens. The choir had finished "Asleep in Jesus." Every seat in the great church was taken. Dr. Lex arose and began the discourse from the text: "Blessed are the dead who die in the Lord." Some twenty minutes was spent showing what was meant by a triumphant departure of one of God's children. Then followed such an eulogy as had never been heard in that church. "Our beloved brother, your beloved pastor has fallen at his post; fallen just as he was about to deliver one of his master sermons on the Savior, whose gospel was so near his heart. I shall always regret that this man was not permitted to be himself during his last moments. Delirium had seized that great brain and the message he left was but shattered fragments of a great soul beating against its prison bars, longing for eternal freedom."

After the sermon was finished the Masonic and Knights Templars, in plumed array, performed these last sad but beautiful ceremonies. "Alas, my Brother"—"Alas, my Brother!"

The sun was disappearing behind the western hills as the last carriage was leaving the scene of interment. The new mound of clay was left buried underneath a thick mantle of flowers. The silence was unbroken but for the evening zephyrs which sang their sad requiems through a tall pine, near by. The eolian harp of early spring kept a lonely vigil over the "bivouac of the dead."

HIGH TIDE AT ROSEVILLE.

CHAPTER I.

"Well, Marth' Ann, I reckon it means four more years of faith and waitin', if the Lord spares us that long," remarked Elijah Brown as he entered the room where his wife, an invalid of several months, was propped up in bed.

"Why, Lijah, what have you heard?" replied the wife in a low, sweet voice; the tone of which told a story of suffering that had been borne with patience and triumph.

"Nothin' special," he said, as he sank into a chair, while a look of sadness closely resembling despair came over his face. "I heard who our new preacher is to be; Col. Staunton read the appointments in a paper at the post-office awhile ago; I never heard the name 'afore as I remember. A lot of the brethren were a shakin' hands over the news; the Colonel said he heard him lecture once at a theater in the city, and he was a No. 1.

"Well, it does seem like we have waited long enough, but the few days we have left are too precious to worry over what we can't help.

This all belongs to the Lord, and I feel like leaving the matter entirely in His hands. We are too old to have any voice in the affairs of our church any more, not even with the official board, much less the cabinet and bishops. He tells us 'all things work together for good to them that love God.' Do you remember a text which Bro. Overton used so much? It was about 'the victory that overcometh the world being *our* faith.'"

"Yes,. yes, I remember, we spent many happy hours with Bro. Overton, and some bright morning I am going to see him again. He crossed over ten years ago, and there's no sort of doubt about where he is today."

Years before this the Rev. Silas Overton, a patient, humble, uncomplaining man of God, had served Central church as pastor, but owing to the opposition of a few leading families, he was removed at the end of one year. He preached the Wesleyan doctrine of entire sanctification, and during the year he taught a few faithful souls the way of life more perfectly, Bro. and Sister Brown being among the number.

Staunton was an Englishman, and a descendent of Lord Fairfax; by far the wealthiest man in Central church, and was the real ap-

New Clothes for the Old Man. 131

pointing power behind the Episcopal throne. No pastor stayed longer than one year who did not pander to the whims of himself and wife. Mrs. Staunton was at heart, a high church Episcopalian. The success of any pastor depended entirely on how he "took" with the Stauntons. No one scarcely dared to even whisper an opinion until a verdict was handed down from the Colonel's mansion. If favorable the new pastor was soon invited to "dine," a little social event which was watched with intense interest by all the membership of Central church.

Colonel Staunton was a representative type of the ante-bellum regime. He stood 6 ft. 4 inches, and walked as straight as a military chieftain on dress parade. His hair and mustache once black as a raven, were now streaked with grey. His stylish dress, spotless linen and cravat, from which shone a large diamond, would naturally impress one that the Colonel was an important personage. In college he had been a class-mate of a leading bishop who often visited at his spacious home. Through this bishop he had access to the entire college of bishops. Hence not only the presiding elder, but the bishops communicated either directly or indirectly with this grandissime of the old school;

notwithstanding he bet heavily on his favorite race horse, figured with the board of trade and boasted of once having fought a duel. He had often stated publicly that he would today avenge an insult on the "field of honor."

"What did you say his name was?" finally asked Mrs. Brown, as her husband was removing the pillows from behind her. "I did not think there was any strange names in our conference."

"He's another transfer," bluntly answered this soldier of three score and ten, "from a church in some other conference; I believe it is Wharton, Dr. Wharton, never heard of him before."

"Well, husband, let us hope as we have been doing so long, that he may be a real shepherd."

"Oh, pshaw!" put in her husband with a slight touch of impatience. Such a word scarcely ever passed his lips, because he walked daily in white before the Lord. "I'm too old to be chasing such a rainbow dream as that! Soon as the Colonel told about his funny lecture I moved on; I didn't want to hear no more."

Elijah Brown and wife were among the charter members of Central church. Forty years ago in the little frame chapel they were made one at its altar. Six children had been dedicated and converted at the same sacred spot. All but a son and daughter who were now living in a distant State, had been carried down its aisle and laid away in Sunny Side Cemetery, south of the town. Notwithstanding the new order of things such as modern annexes, parlors, kitchen, library, choir loft and pipe organ, no place was so near heaven to them as that stately edifice just around the corner from their humble home.

Central church was not the best appointment in the conference, but by far the most important and difficult to fill. It was conceded by all to be the "plumb." For two quadrenniums the pastors had been transfers. Dr Hansome, the last pastor, gave the public a brief account of his work through the columns of the *Advocate* one week before conference. Bro. Brown read this remarkable report to his wife on the evening that their paper came. The following is a part: "Central church is closing four of the greatest years of its history, and it is due my people to say that of thirty years of my itinerant ministry, the years spent with this people are by far the happiest and most successful. When I was appointed here by Bishop ―― there were few over three hundred members, less than one hundred in the Sunday-school and no choir worthy of the name. A heavy parsonage debt was hanging like a pall over the discouraged congregation. Our membership has been doubled; the Lord gave us a gracious revival each year, all financial obligations are met with ease and promptness. Our building is packed at every service. The best musicians of the city belong to our choir. The Sunday-school and all the adjunct societies are the best I ever saw. Our people are loyal and devout, rejoicing in all the doctrines taught and experienced by our beloved Zion. To God be all the glory."

"May the Lord have mercy on us all," she said, turning her sad eyes towards the window through which came a lovely picture of a sunset sky.

It was true the membership had been doubled under the pastorate of Dr. Hansome. Each year an evangelist and singer had been employed, and the meetings were announced by dodgers scattered over town and heavy headlines in the dailies, great flourish of trumpets and eloquent discourses, cards were circulated and signed by the converts; one had actually required them to stand to be counted; another even dared to ask them to come forward and

New Clothes for the Old Man. 135

give their hand to the pastor. It was all a veneering sugar coating process. No altars of prayer, no signs of repentance, no soul agony, no travail, no births by the Spirit, no settling old debts and old trouble, no restitution, no testimony of the saving power of Jesus' blood. Of course such so-called revivals were popular, why not? Any work that does not attack the citadel of Satan—the human heart, is popular with the world, flesh and the devil. Worldliness, pride and selfishness belongs to the unregenerate heart and they will remain until destroyed by repentance and faith in Jesus Christ. Great multitudes were swept into the church, and among them were some of the most aristocratic people of the city. In the lives of many no change had ever been seen. The wine suppers, the whist and euchre clubs, the theater and dance went on unmolested by the pulpit, and undisturbed by any decrease in its number of votaries. The young and beautiful daughter of Dr. Hansome was an acknowledged peer in the *bon ton* circles of Roseville, and often appeared in full evening dress.

How resplendent it all appeared as seen in the conference organ; longing anticipations crept into many hearts when they thought of themselves as likely to get Roseville station.

"This is the Doctor's last year; there must be a change." It was a responsible place but not a few were willing to consecrate themselves to it. At every annual conference the interest usually focalizes around one or two prominent appointments. Every circuit rider seems to be equally interested. At this conference the question was—"who will get Roseville?"

The Doctor's glowing letter had heightened the hopes and ambitions of several "leading brethren."

Uncle Lijah threw the *Advocate* down on the bed, saying as he did so: "Well, what do you think of that, my dear?"

"May the Lord have mercy on us," she repeated, and her large brown eyes wandered about on the scene that became more beautiful as the sun sank below the horizon. Those eyes were once beautiful with the flush of happy young life, and even now all the world seemed to respond and reflect in them, as they traced the lines of that departing autumn day. Tenderness and sympathy were in every look. Already the halo of a glorious dawn was gathering in them. This evening there was a mingling sadness in the shadow that crossed her face; usually there were visible rays of light reflected from a distant shore; now it was a real

New Clothes for the Old Man. 137

shadow, as if caused by a dark object near by. A glimpse into the history of a few weeks previous will reveal the cause of her sadness.

Two weeks before the county fair was held in Roseville. The town was running over with the *rif-raf* from everywhere. Central church always wide-awake and up-to-date could not afford to let such an opportunity pass. The pastor's salary was badly in arrears; seventy-five dollars of the beneficent collections remained unpaid and unprovided for. Consequently a large dining hall was fitted up on the fair grounds. Meals were served by the most beautiful and attractive young women of the Epworth League; also, in connection with this was a "stand," selling all kinds of hot weather refreshments, popcorn and cigars. The secretary of the Epworth League had charge of this part of the concern. To still further replenish the Lord's exchequer an empty store room on a prominent corner in the city was converted into a bazaar, catching the thronging multitudes at night. Here they sold everything from ice-cream to crazy quilts. The week was a tide in the affairs of Central church. Dr. Hansome would have been very much embarrassed at conference, but for the zeal of his "devout people." Those women were satisfied that their zeal for good works would stand a test. The brethren were equally satisfied with themselves on account of their unusual liberality. They had paid twenty-five cents daily for a square meal at the Lord's dining hall, and bought all their cigars from Miss Perkins, the League secretary. This was not all they had done; they actually bought things at the bazaar, that they did not need and used their influence among outsiders, stockmen and race-horse toughs to get their patronage. The success was extraordinary, eclipsing anything in the ecclesiastical history of Roseville. The *Daily Comet* devoted a whole column extolling "those women who labored in the gospel."

The entire ice-cream, pop-corn and crazy quilt business was under the supervision of a Miss Parmelia Tompkins, a general seamstress, hair-dresser, lackey and gossiper for the whole church. Twenty years before she had looked out upon a world all her own, but at last, when too late, she awoke to find herself on her own hands. All the latest freaks and sensations of Central church were always reported promptly to old Brother and Sister Brown.

Personally, she was very fond of the old couple, and she had great respect for their pious

New Clothes for the Old Man. 139

lives, but on real spiritual lines there was nothing in common between them.

This fair supernumerary had gathered all the bits of news about conference, the new preacher, etc., and dropped in on her morning rounds just as Uncle Lijah started to the garden to dig potatoes for dinner, and Jane Wilson, a widowed niece who made her home there, was placing in order her aunt's room.

"Oh, they say we have the finest preacher in the whole church," she almost shouted before she got into the room.

"We've always had the finest according to reports," Aunt Martha replied quickly.

"Yes, but this one is recognized everywhere; a lecture bureau employs all his spare time. We are all just wild to hear him. He won't be here for three weeks, so Col. Staunton said."

"Parmelia, dear, our church needs something besides a lecturer. We are dying with respectability and worldly wisdom. We must offer up something that God will receive before He will ever bless us with a single soul. The second chapter of Joel tells us what we need. I doubt very much if there has been a single conversion in our church for eight years."

"Now, Aunt Martha, you are not feeling so well today. I am sure your fears are without foundation. Dr. Hansome told us the last Sunday, that he doubted if there were a better church in the connection. Why do you always see the dark side of everything?"

"Bless your dear heart, there is no other side to see, when we look at the spiritual condition of our church."

"Dear old soul," thought Miss Parmelia, as she passed out of the gate. "She is so good, but too far behind for these times."

The two weeks in which Dr. Hansome remained in Roseville was one continuous round of receptions and banquets. He was remembered and honored by the Merchants exchange, gentleman's clubs, and all the leading lodges of the city. He belonged to most of these and was very popular.

On Wednesday morning, three weeks after conference, the *Comet* announced the arrival of the Rev. Dr. Wharton, giving a brief sketch of his brilliant ministerial career. He was not seen, however, on the streets with a silk hat and gold-headed cane, as the former's custom had been. No one got to say, "There goes our new pastor." All who passed or called at the parsonage during the week were somewhat surprised to see a small, slender man dressed in

New Clothes for the Old Man. 141

working clothes moving about quietly, unpacking furniture and putting down carpets.

"Oh, but he is all right," they would say. "A man who has a national reputation can afford to do about as he pleases." He's a bit eccentric and perhaps he takes a delight in being odd."

He declined all offers of help, except one man which was hired from the streets.

"Oh, this makes me think of twenty-five years ago when I traveled a circuit at four hundred dollars a year. This work is a part of the inheritance of every itinerant preacher, and I certainly enjoy my part of it," he would say.

Dr. Wharton and wife had been visiting his sister enroute to Roseville, while waiting the slow transportation of the freight. His wife remained to come a week later.

On Thursday morning Colonel Staunton called at the parsonage with much ado of introduction and verbose welcome, also reminding him of the time he lectured at the *Baldwin*. To this reference the pastor seemed to pay no attention. The Colonel was considerably nonplussed as he beheld the little man with sparkling blue eyes shining from a face somewhat dust begrimed, dressed in bib overalls and negligee shirt.

"I'll declare, Rob," he said to his cashier that afternoon, "that preacher stumps me. If I did not know him certainly to be the man that lectured I would never have recognized him. I never enjoyed anything so much. He told more funny stories about the old time, back woods preacher, and shouting Methodists. It was deep, I tell you, as well as funny. He said we were living in the Twentieth century; and old forms, old methods, old creeds, old notions of God and His gospel must be forever laid aside. They came from an age of ignorance and superstition and could no longer be of use to an enlightened people. I tell you he brought the house down."

The Colonel did not turn aside long enough to say that the same delighted audience, himself one of the number, was the identical crowd that had witnessed a scandalous display of nudity the night before, in the same building under the name of "High Class Variety." The high class was low sensational songs almost vulgar, ballet and skirt dancing, girls dressed in a way to stir every devilish passion of depraved human nature. Thousands of Methodists all over the land are nightly visitors to just such entertainments; paying for the same treble the amount they pay to support the Lord's kingdom. Notwithstanding, bishops, and presiding elders often hear their appeals with interest, and wink at the spirit of worldliness that has almost submerged the church, promoting men to the highest places whose ministry stands for nothing but material advancement. Higher criticism no longer debars men from the traveling connection; on the contrary it is an evidence of growing popularity. "The church," they say, "no longer enslaves men's minds and consciences, it has swung away from ultra-conservatism and allows its communicants to be free." Yes, free to be anything, believe anything, and to do anything The worldly minded and devils alike say amen to all such. Parallel and over against such conditions is the *Broad Road* to perdition choked and crowded with communicants of every denomination, passing out from choir lofts, upholstered pews, official boards, ladies aids, Epworth Leagues, and Christian Endeavors. Oh, the cathedral spires, beautiful services, made so by the *Te deums, cantatas,* organ prelude and post-ludes, the ornate pulpit orator, the "safe conservative men" with fat salaries feeding the hungry multitudes on stones, when He who commissions men has spoken in the same voice that shook Sinai, "Ye shall break them the bread of life." Above the rumble of materialism, above the voices prating new creeds, new theologies, new fads, new isms, new psychologies, freedom of thought and humanitarianism sounds out the Word of Him who sits on the throne, "without holiness no man shall see God."

Mr. George Barton, the Sunday-school superintendent, of Central Church, arrived home on Saturday afternoon from a business trip in an adjoining State, and as yet had not met the new pastor. At heart Mr. Barton was a good man; and under proper circumstances would have made a useful man to the cause. He had been converted, but being engrossed with an increasing business, and without spiritual leadership or sympathy, he was very little ahead of the rest. He loved the Sunday-school and was anxious to make it a source of power for good.

"I believe I will drop around and call on our new preacher," he remarked to his wife after supper.

"Well, don't stay long, because I have not asked you half enough questions about the folks back home." Lighting a *Paul Jones* ten cent cigar and putting another in his vest pocket, he walked out wondering if this new preach-

New Clothes for the Old Man. 145

er would like this brand of cigars as well as Dr. Hansome.

Ten minutes walk brought him in sight of the parsonage. Everything was still and dark except a dim light shining from one window. The church was located on a corner with an entrance from both streets. The parsonage was on the opposite side of the block and by passing around to the back yard one could see the window of the pastor's study which was in the rear end of the Sunday-school room. A bright light shone from the study, the evening being warm, the window was raised several inches. Mr. Barton left the brick walk and crossed the lawn to the window, perhaps to peep in before he knocked. He saw a sight that caused him to catch his breath and remain transfixed for a moment. He was accustomed to step in for a few moments' chat with Dr. Hansome on his way down town, and usually found him buried in an easy chair, enjoying his Havana, with feet higher than his head—what did he see? A man lying on his face near the center of the room crying out in agonizing prayer with the eagerness of a child pleading for some desire. The superintendent was so completely dumb-founded that he could not hear the words ,but at intervals caught snatches of sentences. "Father glorify thyself tomorrow," "Send the fire, send the fire, make me a dead man." All this was new phraseology to that man who had worshipped at a Methodist altar for twenty years. Five, ten, fifteen minutes passed and yet the strange scene continued. At the end of half an hour, Mr. Barton who was blameless in life and conversation, a "pillar," walked quietly into the street, overwhelmed by the rush of strange emotions, which he was unable to analyze: surprise, conviction, disgust and reverence were commingled together. When he came to himself his cigar was gone and he forgot the one in his pocket, which was to be the entering wedge of mutual good fellowship with the new pastor.

CHAPTER II.

Mr. Barton was a congenial man in his home, but that night he said nothing and responded to all questions in monosyllables. There was something on his mind

"Wife, something will happen in this town very soon, mark my word," then retired without giving further explanation.

New Clothes for the Old Man. 147

The second bell for Sunday-school was ringing. The superintendent, teachers and pupils were settling down for the opening. Just then Dr. Wharton entered the room from a side door, which lead to the study. But few of the school had seen him. The plainness of his dress and simplicity of his manners attracted the children, and was especially noticed by the fastidious adults.

"Is this Bro. Barton?" he said, coming forward with extended hand. "I am so glad to meet you." Mr. Barton said afterwards that Dr. Wharton's hand-shake went through him like an electric shock. "I simply want to meet your school and then ask you to excuse me this morning until the hour for preaching."

Long before the Sunday-school was over, the auditorium over head was beginning to fill up. At 11 o'clock every seat was taken except the gallery; the greater part of the Sunday-school was compelled to go there. All was hush and expectancy, the great organ began its peals like distant thunder. The pastor entered the pulpit and was almost hid by a profusion of flower-pots sitting on polished brass and bronze tables. Several of these he quietly moved to the back part of the pulpit. This strange performance displeased some and amused others, and interested all. He did not kneel for silent prayer, as was the custom of Dr. Hansome. The first hymn announced was "A Charge to Keep I Have," to the tune of Boylston. He read two stanzas in a soft but penetrating voice.

If the children downstairs were astonished at his modest appearance, imagine the feelings of the aristocratic congregation, when they beheld the pastor of Central Church wearing a sack coat, white linen tie and no watch chain. The opening prayer was a revelation. No more perfunctory, sonorous, sanctimonious, long drawn out platitudes. It was direct, fervent, vigorous and at times wave after wave of melting eloquence swept over the audience. Everything seemed so strange, so unlike anything witnessed in that pulpit before. One man, however, felt that somehow he understood. The picture of that man on his face came into his mind. The words of that prayer: "Gloryfy thyself," "Send the fire," "Make me a dead man," began to unfold a meaning.

The text 1 Cor. 1:30 was announced, "But of him are ye in Christ Jesus, who of God is made unto us wisdom, and righteousness and sanctification and redemption."

There was no flattering complimentary speech made for an opening, as was always ex-

New Colthes for the Old Man. 149

pected. He began the sermon. Notwithstanding his unassuming appearance every one felt that a real man was before them, and one with extraordinary powers. Old Brother Brown had heard all about the unexpected something that was liable to take place and was in a receptive mood for whatever it might be. As the sermon progressed the tide began to rise in his soul; it was a joyous revelation to find an oasis for his thirsty soul. The sermon was divided into four parts, *wisdom, righteousness, sanctification* and *redemption*. At first there was little to attract special attention, except the straight forward, vigorous style of the speaker. The vast audience hung on every word. Under righteousness he began to say things. Christ our righteousness, when we get him every relation in this world must be adjusted to the Decalogue and Sermon on the Mount. Sin in all forms must be forever put away. No compromise; selfishness, covetousness, pride, anger, impure thoughts, lust, envy and unholy ambitions must not be tolerated. For twenty minutes Central Church got volt after volt of divine electricity, such as they never knew existed. The power of God came on the man, his face shone, his eyes blazed while the people held their breath. It was quite obvious that by means of some mysterious agency, the little doctor was an overwhelming majority.

The choir loft was a scene of fidgity uneasiness, but no one dared to stir. If the angel of Jehovah had been walking through that room with a flaming sword the effect would not have been greater. A still greater shock however, awaited them. "He is made unto us sanctification, glory be to His name." Then he proceeded to explain what had been a problem to a greater part of the church for nearly a week. "For sixteen years I have practically selected my own field of labor. Though a Methodist I have been a party to a most unmethodistic custom. A conference transfer is an abomination to the spirit of Methodism. It flatters and feeds pride and worldly ambition. They jump from one fat stall to another, crowding out scores of worthy men in every conference. For sixteen years I have been petted by bishops, flattered by the public with my own advancement uppermost. Chautauquas and lecture bureaus have employed much of my time; another abominable practice for any man to follow who felt a call to the ministry. God pity one who cannot do better with his precious time. En route to this place I visited my only sister in the town of A——. She is a blessed good woman, always my superior spiritually. A holiness camp-meeting was in progress and she entered into the experience of perfect love or sanctification. I prefer the latter name. The precious doctrine is taught in all our standards, but a worldly, ambitious ministry have kept our people out of this the greatest blessing of the Atonement. But this doctrine is true and those who oppose will have to answer at the judgment for the way they have hindered the Holy Ghost in this great work of grace. At last my sister prevailed on me and I went to the camp-meeting. It required but a short time to see that God was in that meeting with power that I had not felt or seen since a boy. It was the gospel of full salvation. My own life came up before me. I saw at least ten years of fruitless ministry, which the world had called unparalelled success. God showed me that in all those years of high living not one soul had really been saved, and I had lorded over his heritage. I had received hundreds into the church without their knowing the initial step of salvation.

"Let me say here that I got a view of that great host of lost souls pointing me out at the judgment and the Rev. J. H. Wharton, D. D. LL.D., author and lecturer, fell at that altar and cried out to God for seven hours. The refining fire came. It was the crucifixion of the "Old Man." I died to this world, and He came, glory to His name, He came. Oh, the joy of full salvation. Oh, the miserable unprofitable ministry of the past. My dear people I have no more time to lose. It was all self, yet I felt like I was honestly serving Christ. 'He is made unto us sanctification.' " For twenty minutes he showed from the scriptures that it was the duty and privilege and the will of God that every believer should be fully sanctified. Excitement, nervousness and disgust were pictured on the face of almost every church member present.

Dr Hansome had preached a series of sermons only a few months before which had fully explained this doctrine to the satisfaction of every dancer and card player in the church.

It was anything but a dull occasion. Miss Parmelia was almost in convulsions; some were almost ready to faint, others were in a perfect rage. Bro. Brown was the one person who indorsed fully the entire program. Every time he gave vent to an amen, fifty people would look him through with daggerous eyes. The sermon had lasted one hour. "We shall not discuss," he said, "the last division; it is not

New Clothes for the Old Man. 153

necessary to worry over final redemption until we attend to wisdom, righteousness and sanctification. Services tonight; are there any announcements, brethren?"

"Yes, sir," almost shouted Col. Staunton. "I want to meet the members of the official board in my study tomorrow evening at 8 o'clock. This is for the official board *only*," with much emphasis on the only. "There are some important matters to be discussed touching the interests in Central Church." His face was pale and his body trembled with emotion. Very few pressed forward to speak to Dr. Wharton after the benediction. All was confusion, little knots of people were gathered here and there in the room muttering in tones of subdued passion. Miss Parmelia almost ran around the corner to see Sister Brown. All out of breath she poured forth a perfect volley of inarticulate words. "An *awful* sermon," "perfectly horrid," "holiness crank," "our church is just ruined," "Col. Staunton is so mad," "they'll make him leave," etc. To all this unintelligible mouthing, Sister Brown listened quietly, but there came a flush of joy into her face, and a strange light into her eyes that even her excited tormentor did not fail to see; all she said was, "Praise the Lord, at last, at last." In a moment Miss Parmelia rushed out to gain audience with some one else and in came Bro. Brown clapping his hands and rejoicing, "Oh, Martha Ann, he's come at last. We will spend this noon hour thanking God for sending us a shepherd. Come, Jane, cover up the table," putting his head into the kitchen door. "We won't eat just now." What a prayer-meeting, what a praise service. "Miss Parmelia tried to tell me about the Colonel but I could not understand her. Tell me about it all."

He related the whole service in detail from beginning to end.

"Well, God can take care of his servants and his work, too," she remarked, "and I am inclined to leave the Colonel and this whole matter with Him."

The hour for evening service had arrived. The league had been dull and uninteresting. Every ones mind was full of the events of the day and the expectations of the coming service.

Central Church seated comfortably six hundred people, and all available space was occupied by others standing, while many were turned away. At the exact moment the little doctor calmly entered the pulpit and began the service with as much composure as an old-time

New Clothes for the Old Man. 155

circuit rider would at the farthest point on "Post Oak Circuit."

"I shall endeavor to bring you a message tonight from two passages from God's word. First, "Whosoever, therefore will be a friend to the world is an enemy to God." Second, "And the wicked shall be turned into hell, with all the nations that forget God."

For over an hour he uncovered sin and its consequences. They who thought the morning sermon terrible, realized that it was only a foretaste of what they were hearing then. The bottomless pit seemed to yawn before their eyes, the church and congregation felt that nothing on earth could prevent them from slipping in. Strong men trembled like leaves. The effect was indescribable. Young men and women were literally frightened as in present danger. The judgment day was upon them and they were doomed. Women of high social rank began to stammer and whisper confessions to each other, and to their husbands if near together. Hundreds of resolutions of confessions and restitution were fermenting the souls of that breathless audience. At last the preacher shouted, "All who desire to get right with God tonight, come to this altar." At least two dozen actually fell at the altar of that church where no penitent had knelt seeking the Lord for many years. One came from the gallery and one came from the choir. The pastor prayed and talked to the penitents, and a goodly number found pardon and arose with shining faces.

The surprise was overwhelming when the preacher announced meeting for Monday night. After the congregation was dismissed they stood looking at each other as if not knowing whether to go home or remain.

If all that was said and thought on the streets and in the homes of Roseville, could have been written it would be a large and interesting volume. Everybody was talking about the preacher and his meeting. Colonel Staunton worked several hours preparing a paper, which, when signed by the official board, was to be forwarded to the bishop. In substance it was an ultimatum for the removal of Dr. Wharton from Roseville.

They met and a story meeting it was. Only one member was willing to sign the resolution, and that man rented a building from the Colonel in which he run a small grocery store, and at that time was owing the Colonel several hundred dollars. Of course he was willing. The rest flatly refused, a thing no

New Clothes for the Old Man. 157

one had ever before dared to do, if that man requested it. Some how the day before had wrought a work in the minds at least of those men which gave them courage, to overrule for once, the czar of Central Church. One by one they would say, "Brethren, will you excuse me, please, I want to go to church," and finally Colonel Staunton was left to nurse his rage alone. His defeat was humiliating, and no one felt the defeat more keenly than Mrs. Staunton. Her health began to fail rapidly, and without further council or communication with the pastor or people, the Colonel and wife started for Florida ten days later, to spend the winter.

Miss Parmelia was also called away very soon to visit a dear(?) aunt and was not seen in Central Church again for many months.

Another important thing happened on that Monday after the volcanic explosion. Sister Brown was suddenly taken worse about nine o'clock, and Dr. Wharton was sent for. He was not specially wanted to administer comfort, for that One, whose bleeding foot-prints she had so long been following was there to take part in the last scene. The room was pervaded by His glorious presence, the very stillness itself echoed with voices from beyond the river. She held out a thin white hand to her pastor, saying: "I wanted to see you before I go. God has at last answered my prayer. Now that the Ark is moving forward I am ready. The sky was never so bright as this morning No clouds in sight, the waters are breaking around my feet, but I am so happy. By faith I see a bright angel getting my robe out of the heavenly wardrobe. Dear pastor, I just know it is mine to wear very soon."

For an hour this holy communion of saints lasted, then she said, "Come to me, dear husband, for I am going now. Don't be lonesome; I will watch for you daily. He saves now, bless His holy name. Dear Brother Wharton, be true to God, keep all on the altar, die daily and all will be well. Jane, dear child, come and kiss me, you have been so good and patient. Oh, it is growing so dark. It cannot be that the day has passed so soon and the sun setting. Oh, so dark, I cannot see you, but look at that beautiful light. Oh, the gospel is true and I see the upper lights of glory," and that soul leaped from the prison of pain and suffering to roam forever in the Paradise of God.

Jane was sobbing on one side of the bed, and on the other the husband was praising the Sav-

New Clothes for the Old Man. 159

ior for salvation that would destroy the sting of death, while the pastor stood silently watching the triumphant ending of God's sanctified child.

A throng of people gathered at Central church on Tuesday evening to attend the funeral of one who amid worldliness and unbelief had walked in the white garments of holiness for a quarter of a century. She was buried beside her sleeping children in Sunny Side Cemetery. Her beloved church was at last in reality what it had been to her so long by faith, "the gates of heaven to her waiting soul."

On that quiet, sunny October day, the heavens seemed to stoop very low as the multitude watched the little mound rise up over the form of Aunt Martha Brown.

The revival which began with services on Sunday night swept on. About one hundred and fifty members of Central church were saved, and an equal number outside of the church. Three pastors of the city entered into the Canaan experience; editors, lawyers, doctors, bankers, society men and women alike went down under the power. Other churches took up the meeting under sanctified leadership, and the revival lasted throughout the winter.

Saloons were driven out, the dancing academy shut down, and the theatre manager lost money continually. The news spread over the country. The gamblers steered clear of Roseville. When the spring primary election came on, the citizens nominated a full ticket, which was elected by a strong majority. A political ring had controlled the town for years. Mr. Barton was elected mayor; three councilmen were also members of Dr. Wharton's church. The beer garden and Sunday base ball were not permitted that season. Real estate almost doubled in value; business in all lines flourished. The Lord God Almighty ruled and reigned in the people of Roseville. The tide so long delayed came in at last ladened with rich treasures, and sorrow and sighing had flown as if on the wings of morning.

SIN'S LEGACY.

CHAPTER I.

The wedding of Rev. Claud Randall, the young and gifted pastor of Plymouth Methodist church, was to be the principal social function of the season. He was entering upon the third year of his first pastorate; though scarcely thirty years of age, large crowds gathered each Sabbath to hear his eloquent discourses. He had attracted some attention while in college as a winner of the inter-collegiate oratorical contest. Very early in his ministry it was known by the bishop that young Randall was a "safe, conservative man," and his pleasing address had received favorable mention in the *Advocate* as a prospective *transfer*. "The eye of the church" is running to and fro, seeking such rare combinations. In college he was considered really religious by his companions, but on rereiving one of the best pulpits in the conference, when admitted on trial, proved by no means an advantage to his piety. From such dizzy heights hundreds of splendid young men have caught the mirage of coveted place and honor, consequently becoming dumb to the higher claims of the ministry. However, the young pastor tried to be conscientious and honest, but success and much flattery, Satan's strongest leverage on unmarried preachers, had bleared the high ideals of his earlier years.

There were at least a score of marriageable young women among the membership of Plymouth church, but the beautiful and accomplished daughter of Judge Burbank proved to be the one chosen "Mistress of the Manse." The young preacher can select but one, but when that one is selected it always causes more or less comments and criticisms. Why *she* should be the one is the problem in the mind of every suitable candidate or their anxious and envious mothers. In the social and domestic circles may be heard such remarks as: "Well, I am sure I don't want him," and "I always said my girl should never marry a preacher, if I could prevent it," etc. All of which is very amusing to the sensible brethren and sisters who believe that even a preacher should have the right to woo and wed the lady of his choice.

Judge Burbank was an official member of the church, and very prominent in financial and political circles. His religion consisted more of inherited afflliations than any real experience or convictions; he would fight for the church, but was not willing to give up the least selfish indulgence for the Master. No man wielded more influence in state politics than he, and his popularity among the vicious element was an evident fact, as they gave him no trouble and he gave them none.

Luella, the only daughter, had been given every advantage that wealth and social position could offer. Her musical education was completed at an Eastern conservatory. When it was known that Luella Burbank was to sing a solo on Sunday, the music loving people from other churches would attend the services. The father was not at all elated over the approaching wedding. Such a life must necessarily debar her from social triumphs so easily attainable by one so beautiful and bright as his daughter. Mrs. Burbank, being a good Christian woman, with an unusual amount of common sense, was actually delighted that her only daughter was to be the wife of a minister of her beloved Zion. The Judge was not insensible to the growing popularity of the man who had won his daughter's heart. Besides, his conduct had been that of a true man; noble in every respect. In his heart he admired the young man above all others, but could not help contrasting the life of an itinerant with that of Clifford Grayson, who being already well to do, had recently inherited his uncle's entire estate of one hundred and fifty thousand dollars. Clifford and Luella had been playmates since infancy, and now he loved her to desperation. Not until the wedding was announced did he cease to press his claim and hope. She pitied him and treated his passionate appeals with kindness, which always gave him more or less encouragement. The thought of being defeated in a heart contest by a "poor preacher" was too humiliating for this young nabob, so he departed for California in a few days after the matter became known.

There were two children of the Burbank family, one son two years older than Luella. John Burbank had many good qualities, though he treated religion with supreme indifference, much to the sorrow of his sister, who was far in advance, religiously, of the young women in her circle. Since her association with the young minister she had withdrawn entirely from the worldliness that was so bold and blatant in all the leading churches of Plymouth. John rarely attended church, though he was very fond of Mr. Randall. His associations were the sports of town, and his headquarters "Sportman's Club House." Notwithstanding, he loved his sister dearly and esteemed her highly for what he considered "piety unto martyrdom," viz: to be the wife of a Methodist preacher. He and Clifford Grayson had been chums for years. John often acting as a go-between for him and Luella. Since Mr. Grayson became heir to much wealth, he led a fast, dissipated life, but these facts were not known outside the club circle. John Burbank cared very little for churches or preachers, but somehow he felt relieved when he knew that his companion in sin had been rejected as a suitor by his lovely sister·

The date announced for the nuptials was July 4. The official board had granted the pastor one month's vacation, during July, which was done at the suggestion of Dr. Sims, the P. E.

Congratulations were coming in from all sides. Every mail brought messages from interested friends of the young pastor, and his life seemed to be under a special benediction. Every avenue before him assumed a roseate glamour. Sometimes, however, when in the silence of his own chamber, a "still small voice" would whisper into the deep of his soul, "What does all this mean to Me? Am I to be glorified in this splendid triumph? Is it not I who called you into my vineyard?" All such voices were easily drowned by the emotions that flooded every aspiration of his being. Then, after all, wherein was the harm? He had not sought Luella's hand because she was rich. It was an helpmeet he wanted and had found her. All this honor came unsought. Was it not all from the Lord because of his faithfulness? But these voices continued to clamor, and at times a stone seemed to be hanging to his heart. Questions would float through his mind, from which he would deduce a soliloquy, "Would all this have come to me, had I been absolutely true to my highest convictions? Would this proud, fashionable people love and honor me if I should preach the Word in its fulness? Does this people know anything about the regenerated life; do they bear any real fruits of the Christ likeness? They pay all the church obligations, but this is not more than one or two per cent of what they ought to pay. In the light of my own conscience can I address them as saved people; with but few exceptions, there is no difference in the lives of my people and the unbelieving, unregenerated world about us." But when a new day broke on his horizon, all

New Clothes for the old Man. 167

such troublesome hallucinations would depart and all was peace again within. "I was a little blue last night," he would remark to himself. "How foolish we are to allow such extravagant phantasms to disturb us. If all was not right, the Lord would not bless and prosper me as He does." Thus the ever ready opiate did its perfect work. Thus ambitions as earthly as ever fired the brain of Caesar rose a little higher each time like an incoming tide, sweeping this brilliant young man further and further from conscience and God.

Three weeks before the wedding day, Rev. Randall and Miss Burbank were returning from a drive a few miles out on the pike, when, by chance, they left the main street, leading toward home, to make a short call in another part of the city. The long June day was drawing to a close; a lovely sunset, that flooded the ragged cloud-land with gold and vermilion, and bathed the landscape with a noonday brightness, had enhanced the glow and fervency of their own souls, blending their lives with hope, ennobling and pure.

One week previous to this an unknown evangelist had begun a meeting in a little Free Methodist church located near the part of town which Miss Hegan would call a "cabbage patch," through which the lovers must pass to reach the house of their friend. A brief announcement of the meeting appeared in the papers, but received scarcely a passing notice.

"By the way," said he, "here is the church where the evangelist is holding forth. Suppose we take it in, and call on Miss Larkum on Thursday evening; we drive then, you know"

"The very idea," answered Luella, "our friends will enjoy a laugh at our expense if they find it out; I hear they are good, simple hearted people. But we are too late, are we not?"

"A little late, but I don't suppose we will have any trouble to get a seat:" In this he was mistaken. They found the little frame building crowded, and many standing at the windows outside. All the furnishings were of the plainest and cheapest. What a contrast to the upholstered pews, carpeted floor, pipe organ, and polished chandeliers. Where all these things were lacking, there was something else far more valuable. On the faces of many was a luster and radiance of ineffable brightness. Mr. Randall was at once recognized, being a pastor, whereupon room was made for them near the front. He was invited to sit in

New Clothes for the Old Man. 169

the pulpit, but kindly declined. "What will you do when the shouting begins," he whispered in Luella's ear. "Goodness!" she almost exclaimed out loud, "do you think they will?"

"Very likely, if the preacher gets off all right."

"Dear me, I wish we had not come," Luella said nervously.

The unpretentious, and plainly dressed evangelist took for a text, James 4:8: "Cleanse your hands ye sinners, purify your hearts ye double minded." A new text and a little strange, so the visiting preacher was deeply interested in a few moments, notwithstanding the inelegance of the whole occasion.

The first part was a stirring appeal to the unsaved. It was very unusual, the way he addressed the sinners. Sin was not a mistake, but an awful, ruinous blight. They were lost —no hope, no future but death and eternal darkness. Though rich and cultured, they were under the power of Satan Respectability or church membership was not less lost. LOST. *Lost.* LOST. This word rang through Luella's soul in a strange way. "Ye must be born again." Without it no power on earth or heaven could save.

There was much curiosity in the mind of

Rev. Randall as to what he would say about the "double minded." Not one word had yet been said about that part of the text. The double minded were God's people who had not been delivered from the carnal mind. They were born again, but lacked full deliverance. The best men and women in the church were shown to be double minded. Never did a sermon carry such conviction to any as this one did to that young preacher who thought he was sincere, but found himself mistaken. Many times had the Holy Spirit whispered these same things to his heart. Double minded! Yes, even more than he had ever dreamed. Self had shared more than half of his time, thought, and meditations. Here was a direct command from God's word. As the first part had stirred the foundations of Luella's soul, so had the latter touched her companion in a marvelous manner. At the close an altar call was made for sinners—the lost, and many went forward and fell upon their knees and began to call on God for help. Luella never witnessed such a sight in her life, though reared in a Methodist church, and had attended its "revivals" each year. Then a different call was made for those who wanted to be entirely cleansed from sin, so they could love God with their whole

New Clothes for the Old man.   171

heart, and live absolutely surrendered to His will. Many went forward, seeking this experience at the same altar where the sinners were weeping and praying. The fight waxed warmre and warmer, so that our friends made their exit the very first opportunity.

"Oh dear," sighed Luella, as he assisted her into the phaeton, I never want to come to such a place again." Wasn't he simply awful? Why, I am almost excited out of my wits."

"I never witnessed anything like it in *my* life," said this Methodist preacher who had the college and seminary finish on all his ministry.

They rode home in silence; very few words were exchanged. Both hearts were struggling with new, strange emotions, unlike anything they had ever experienced. Somehow all the poetry had gone out of the beautiful moonlight; nothing was said about the approaching honey-moon. Their love for each other, so pure and enchanting, was forgotten when under the sway of higher and holier influences. The Holy Spirit was wooing them in the dark valley of conviction to paths which lead through green pastures beside the still waters.

A Gethsemane awaited each, when they

retired for the night in their chambers alone. In bitterness each cried out for the cup to pass. Hour after hour swept by as if on the wings of the wind, and yet dragging and galling like the heavy chains of death. Sleep departed. Had each one known the terrible struggle going on in the other's soul, there would have been doubtless a victory gained so radical and wonderful that not only the town of Plymouth, but the entire church would have felt the shock. But Satan, ever on the alert, blinds the eyes of honest souls, and if possible hedges up the way of the determined. It was the wrestling of Jabbock repeated over again, but from the anguish and rebellion of Luella, the Nazarene departed. "Go thy way, but oh come at a more convenient season." The near future was too precious to her. Egypt, with its pyramids, flesh pots, dancing maidens, and swing gardens never before cast such a spectrum on the retina of her imagination. Diabolus conqueror. The gates of the world swung wider open than ever, music weird, voluptious, floated over that midnight drama. The King's Highway seemed strangely to vanish in the hazy distance. Poor soul, could she have but felt or known how much sorrow was involved in that decision; oh, the despair that must be felt, so near, yet hovering away under the pall of the unknown. Oh the wormwood and gall that her proud lips must taste before another day-star will appear. Could the veil have been withdrawn for one moment, the peaceful repose of those remaining hours would have been spent in travail unto death.

In Mr. Randall's room the struggle continued until friendly sunbeams peeked in through the lattice and honey-suckle, telling him that God had not forgotten the world. His soul was tossing upon a raging sea without helm or compass, far beyond the sight of haven or land. The frolics of the bee and humming bird about his window had lost their gladsomeness of yesterday. The day was spent in silence and alone, but night found him seated among those poor and despised worshipers with a look of desperation in every line of his countenance. Though poor, he knew they were drinking at a Fountain of exhaustless wealth; thus he returned, poor, troubled soul, believing there was room at the same Fountain for him.

CHAPTER II.

Never before had this young minister felt the presence of so many kind, sympathizing friends as he did during the hour that he spent agonizing on his knees, crucifying the "old man" of sin. Oh, how dark seemed all the world to him now. Oh, the fervent prayers that ascended from that humble "bench," such holding on to God by those unlearned, unsophisticated workers at the altar.

"Jist keep diggin' brother, when you git to the bottom you'll know it," and many other such remarks were spoken in his ears.

Just as the atonement of Christ is universal and unlimited, so is the ambition and purpose of Satan universal. He allows no one freedom from sin without a protest as violent as his fiendish character can invent. No one has an easy time getting into full salvation. It is the pearl of great price and whoever gets it must sell all that he hath. Consecration is a very popular and easy subject to preach and write about, but when we really undertake to make an offering of self, it becomes a most serious business, and very few, when face to face with what it involves, have the courage to make it. It means a literal crucifixion in every way re-

New Clothes for the Old Man. 175

sembling the crucifixion of Christ, except the nailing of the body to a cross. The crucifixion must be two-fold, viz: we to the world and the world to us. Many imagine that the work is done in them as a result of a superficial consecration, but the humiliation and defeat that often follows, reflects sadly upon the possibilities of what there is in the atonement for those who will dare meet the conditions fully. Of all who undertake to sweep into this blessed experience, no one has such a death as the ambitious young preacher, with the prestige of college training and the favor of the "powers" behind him. The ordination vows demand that he shall do this thing, but it means Anathama Maranatha to the preacher who gets it. Herein lies a problem, so profound that it baffles the wisdom of sages and saints. That men, chief shepherds and other lesser bosses, should stultify and coerce the consciences of their brethren, who are in every way as capable and worthy, simply because they differ with them. This problem becomes more stupendous when we remember our church is committed to this precious doctrine in all her standards. The preacher who refuses to push on into perfect love and get it, or denies the doctrine, ignores his ordination vows and puts his wisdom over against our founders of Methodism and rejects the theology from Wesley down, with scarcely an exception. Even some leaders who are known more for their ability to "stamp out this modern craze" than for any souls saved under their ministry, are forced to ackuowledge it a Wesleyan doctrine, or advertise themselves as either ignorant or dishonest. To the young minister it means certain disfavor with the appointing powers; branded as cranky and fanatical; a walk through life more or less lonely, as this world, though joined to a church, or rather an ecclesiasticism is not moving on "the straight and narrow way," and they do not propose to; and whoever puts himself against such a current will very soon learn what it means to live "Godly in Christ Jesus." It means that he can no longer expect to preach in the best pulpits, the wealthy and cultured do not want that kind of prophesying; the cry goes up that such a ministry "divides," "splits" and "ruins." It divides, splits and ruins because when presented it implies the awful doctrine of sin and its consequences. Such messages always find some who want to "flee from the wrath to come" and some who do not It divides just as impenitence and sin are divided from penitence and a hungering for righteousness.

The unsanctified heart though suppressed by much prayer and faith has *carnality*, which contains the germ of every sin in the decalogue. This is Satan's home in "*Man soul*," and so long as he remains there is interval warfare, fierce and bitter. Oh, how many have been lost in this great tragedy of life because he was not forced to move outside the walls of man soul. A holy life, a holy gospel, a Holy Ghost are an offence to a heart dominated by the carnal mind. "*It is not subject to the law of God.*"

The whole problem of persecution, opposition, and rejection of this doctrine, so graciously promised in God's word, can be solved by a clear understanding of the carnal mind. This is the "old man" of sin which Paul says must be crucified.

Claude Randall had counted the cost and was determined to sell all he had. The Spirit had clearly revealed to him that nothing short of this would gain the "pearl." Among the workers at the altar was a bright eyed, sweet faced girl, who was kneeling near the young preacher.

She portrayed culture and refinement far above her humble brethren and sisters, among whom she seemed to worship with perfect harmony. Her dress was plain but neat. She had attracted his attention the night before, owing to the marked contrast she bore to those about her. Stooping close to his ear she whispered: "Are you willing to pay the price?" These words were spoken with an intuition that was remarkable. He was the pastor of a fashionable, worldly church, and soon to be married into one of her leading families. These facts were known by all who kept up with the happenings through the dailies. His deep earnestness had not escaped the keen eyes of Grace Daniels.

That night found him there alone; no one took in the situation like she, as the higher circle of Plymouth church was known personally to her. Only since her experience of full salvation had she withdrawn from it. Somehow, she felt that she knew. "God help me," groaned the man. She listened and prayed, "Are you willing that God should have His way with you?" she said again very softly. "Will you say yes *now* to all He would have you do?" The preacher's breath came in gasps; sweat stood out in great beads on his forehead; his body shook like a whirlwind playing on a summer pool; every function of his soul was agitated beyond control.

"Are you ready now?" she repeated gently. "Remember He suffered without the gate, and trod the winepress alone, and are you willing to stand where He stood, bearing His reproach?"

He raised his head and looked at the sweet little face near him; his eyes wild and glassy. "Yes, I will *here and now*," he answered, in a voice resembling the growl of an animal at bay. At this point the workers began with power and unction. "Is not this the land of Beulah." He leaped to his feet and shouted: "Yes, glory, hallelujah," with a glow on his face, such as Moses had coming down from the Mount. "O, I can not stand it. I can not stand it; the fire is burning me up. I shall die, glory, glory."

"Jis' let'er burn, brother," said the simple-hearted old man who had been talking to him before Grace Daniel arose from her knees with a halo of celestial light around her beautiful face. "Thank God, another witness in our town," she said to herself.

For almost an hour Claude Randall shouted, sang, shook hands, and talked to the seekers. Many more were converted and sanctified that night. Oh, if the fastidious members of Plymouth church could have looked upon that scene; their pastor once so cautious of every pronunciation, posture, and style, now in the full swing of those crazy Free Methodists.

At the close of the service Grace Daniels gave the minister her hand and said, "Good night; God bless you. The Lord will help you to meet the situation, and I will pray for you." Neither of them ever dreamed of how much was involved in that "situation," to which she had just referred. His only answer was an overflow of joy: "Bless the Lord, I am so happy."

Another scene was transpiring at the same time; not a Gethsemane, not a Calvary. Two vessels very near each other can drift into opposite currents and in a few hours the horizon may be between them. Thus it was with Mr. Randall and his betrothed. Only a few hours before they were united by bonds which seemed to be holy and eternal; but now, though they knew it not, an infinity lay between them; a yawning chasm deep and wide, heaven and hell, time, eternity!

Luella received a call that evening from Miss Lucile Gravier, a social fixture of Plymouth, whose ancestors, being of the nobility, had fled from France during the Reign of Terror. Luella gave a detailed account of her experience the evening before, with all her wit and enthusiasm added "And do you believe me, Mr. Claude really looked sober over the affair." Both girls laughed heartily over such "wild perversions." Miss Gravier was more Catholic than anything else, but would attend anywhere that an attraction was offered. Religion to her was little better than a joke. Before she entered her carriage, she had gained a promise from Luella to attend a reception to be given by her the next week, in honor of a dancing professor and his wife that were leaving Plymouth. Luella was astonished at herself in a few moments afterwards, as she had not been seen in such company for over a year. The "crest" was to be there! the votaries of fashion, the prize winners at progressive euchre, the dancers, the theatre-goers, Sabbath desecrators, moral lepers, both men and women; the legitimate sequence of social life. Luella excused herself on the grounds that it would *never* occur again, as she was soon to be forever removed from such phases of life. How was such a compromise possible to one who had made so many good resolutions of service and usefulness. The answer lies far beneath the meshes of anything visible. A Stranger had knocked the night before, one that had guarded and hovered about the life so full of promise as was hers; but He was refused admission. With that refusal the Stranger departed, and that departure carried a loss so great that years of sorrow and wretchedness could not comprehend it all.

Early the next morning Luella received a note from Claude which ran as follows:

"My dearest, with a heart full to overflowing, I send my greetings, as I can not see you face to face. Oh, Luella, I can not tell you, words fail me utterly, but I have joy in my soul that is truly 'past understanding.' Christ in His fulness and sanctifying power is abiding with me continually. We have such a precious Savior. He is mine, yours. A new song is leaping up in my heart, and all the world is full of harmony. I now understand the wonderful gospel we heard last night. Will see you at four this evening CLAUDE."

This message sent a pang to her heart; she stood for a moment like one dazed and blinded. Then as if walking from a reverie, she tore the note into tiny bits, flung herself on a sofa and began to sob bitterly. What an opportunity for the Evil One who is always seeking entrance where least suspected. Every hateful, rebellious spirit of which depraved nature is heir swept her away like a flood. We may educate, refine, moralize, and humanize the unregenerated soul, even if it be an exponent of the beautiful and true, but when a moment of supreme test comes, the den of wild beasts, hateful birds and creeping things will burst the prison bars and destroy the prison. As the hours passed the flame in her soul fanned by the rulers of darkness became a conflagration. By three o'clock her passion had not in the least calmed, as indicated by the following note which she sent to her lover:

"Rev Claude Randall:

"I can not drive this evening. I am sick and do not wish to see any one. Do not call until you hear from me .   LUELLA."

"This is a part of the price," he muttered to himself, as he re-read the strange lines so unkind and so full of meaning; a meaning that no one knew so well as he. What a test! Who can sound the depths of Satan's iniquity when bent on the wrecking of human souls. How infamous his suggestions and his ways past finding out. He went to his room with the unfaltering trust of a child, and fell upon his knees: "O Father, Thou knowest all. Show me from Thy word the message I need." He opened at Isa. 26:3, "Thou will keep him in perfect peace whose mind is staid on thee."

It was walking through the fiery furnace accompanied by one like unto the Son of God. Joy, peace, praise, and thanksgiving coursed through his soul until he felt that he must ask the Father to remove His hand.

The second day passed and no word came from Luella. He sent a beautiful bouquet of roses and carnations, but no response. They were to be married in three weeks. Was he to be rejected now, without a word of explanation.

The news of what had occurred reached the daily press, though he had told no one but Luella. The leading daily in an adjoining city gave it much publicity, in bold head lines. *"Brilliant young pastor converted to holiness. Will doubtless resign his pulpit. Soon to have been married to a beautiful heiress. May break the engagement. Great sensation in religious circles of Plymouth. Thought by official board to be insane,"* etc., etc.

This "write up" was from the home of Dr. Sims, the P. E. On Saturday a letter came to Rev. C. Randell bearing a special delivery stamp. He recognized the writing to be that of Dr. Sims. He opened it slowly and read: "My Dear Claude—

"I herewith enclose a clipping from the

Chronicle which explains itself. I am distressed and pained more than I can tell. My prayer is that there may be some mistake. No young man in our church had brighter prospects. Should this report be true or any part of it, I regard the affair as nothing less than a calamity. Will be up Monday, Cordially,
 "THOMAS SIMS."

Looking at the floor dreamily for a moment he placed the letter in his pocket and said to himself, "Pearls are always expensive. The greatest pearl must mean the greatest price. I am paying another installment. Hallelujah!"

About twenty minutes after this remarkable letter arrived, the long-looked for note came from Luella. Mr. Randall had become almost prepared for any surprise, but this one was unusual, unexpected. It was brief and the real message was portrayed in what was not written. Like many spoken words the meaning can only be found in the unsaid.

"My Dear Mr. Randell: I write to inform you that owing to unlooked for circumstances our wedding must be postponed, perhaps indefinitely. Dr. Jordan advises a change and I shall start tomorrow night for the lakes and will remain during the hot season. Many

thanks for the flowers you sent. They were lovely. Will I see you before I go?
                                    Kindly, LUELLA."

This went like an arrow to his heart, and he groaned in spirit for a moment, because he took in the full import of what the *change* meant to him. Then he remembered, "All things work together for good to them that love God." He knew the *change* had already taken place. His spiritual discernment was acute and he knew better than she or the doctor what was needed. However, he resolved at once to call at Judge Burbank's home. We are not permitted to hear the words of that interview, touching Luella's strange conduct, but an hour later the young preacher left the house with a look of triumph on his face, fully determined to forsake houses, lands, parents and wives that he be worthy of the Nazarene.

Luella started on Sunday for the indefinite journey. A week before she could not have been induced to desecrate the Sabbath in any way. When once Satan had gained access to the heart, he takes possession of the entire citadel. She had crossed the border line of the inheritance which sin offers as a legacy to every one who will reject the Christ

The news of Plymouth's young pastor being converted to "holiness" had truly created quite a stir among the membership, yet very little had been said. Standing room was at a premium Sunday morning. There was nothing unusual in the preacher's appearance. His sermon was delivered with a passion of fervor that had never characterized him before. Then it was ornate eloquence, with finished climaxes; now it was spontaneous eloquence on fire with the Holy Ghost Every one recognized the change, but every one was fortified against the "fanaticism" which they were sure was going to be let loose among them. At the close he stepped to the side of the pulpit and told the breathless congregation of what the Lord had done for him in a tone of humility and meekness. Since the days of the weeping Jeremiah, tears were never shed on a colder and more irresponsive congregation. Judge Burbank attended the service that morning to know for himself, and he walked out after the benediction stiff and determined.

"Daughter," he remarked at the table, "I would not allow you to do a dishonorable thing, but I heartily coincide with your views and congratulate your wisdom. You are justifiable in breaking your engagement with Mr. Randall. You may remain away a whole year if you choose. I am so sorry, so sorry it happened." In his voice was a ring of insincerity which his wife recognized; she knew that her husband was rejoicing in his heart. She had pleaded in vain with Luella. For the first time in life she had heeded the advice of her father against her mother. Another point for Satan. Mrs. Burbank believed in young Randall and his experience. Down in her own soul had always been a hungering for the "well of water springing up." To her it was fighting the Holy Ghost, and with an eye of faith she saw as did the Master from the brow of Olives an awful day of retribution. It came, and that speedily.

CHAPTER III.

Much of the stir and excitement incident to what was recorded in the previous chapter got into the local press, thence to a wider circulation. A copy of some paper giving briefly the whole story fell into the hands of Clifford Grayson. A letter of inquiry came to Plymouth by the first mail, and it was written to one capable of giving the answer all the necessary color;

also definite information as to the whereabouts of Luella Burbank. In less than two weeks, this young sport, devoid of every moral qualification except "appearance," was promenading with Luella amid the grounds of a fashionable summer resort on the shore of a northern lake.

"My, my," she said with a slight effort at jollity, "what changes can come in a few days! In one week was to be my wedding—and then the "Mistress of the Manse."

"At one thousand a year," laughed Clifford.

"Gracious! but I am almost glad I escaped."

"But, come, now," he urged, "are you not truly glad? Think of the life of hum-drum drudgery. You were never intended for such a narrow sphere. Let those do such things who are not capable of doing anything better."

They were soon seated under a beautiful arbor, when the glare of an electric light shone through an opening, revealing her bare neck and arms and the full luster of her large, hazel eyes. The blazing eyes of an animal, ready to spring upon its victim, never feasted with deeper or more dangerous desire than did the eyes of this dissolute young man as he gazed upon this poor, deluded girl, who, unconscious of her awful danger, was as beautiful as a dream.

He pressed her hand gently and spoke in a deep undertone. "May I have my answer tonight, darling?"

She trembled, a pallor spreading over her face. "No, no; not now. I feel that I am not entirely released from Mr. Randall. Somehow I feel nervous and chilly. Let us go in; we will talk of this matter tomorrow."

Falling on his knees and grasping both her hands, he spoke in desperation: "You must *not* go until you promise to be my wife· I can give anything—everything—to make you happy. I will take you to Europe, if you want to go."

"Do you really love me so, Clifford?"

"Do I? How could you taunt me with such a question?"

"Then I promise, but will make no arrangements until I have communicated with Mr. Randall. I can not act dishonorably." A gentle breeze came sighing through the foliage above them, whispering the ominous prophecy of an overshadowing fate soon to chill her guilty but misguided heart.

From the balcony of the hotel came floating out through the soft evening air the beautiful strains of Lang's *Flower Song*, played by the orchestra. It was truly an overture, which

New Clothes for the Old Man.   191

preceded the ascending curtain upon what promises to be a charming drama, but was indeed a tragedy, and the first scene was when Luella Burbank placed her hand in the hand of Clifford Grayson with a promise to be his wife.

Luella soon excused herself, and once in her room it began to dawn upon her what was involved in the promise just made. Every good resolution and desire that she had made since her engagement to Mr. Randall came crowding into her mind, and seemed to hover over her bed like a brood of taunting, hissing demons. All night long she tossed and wept. The face of her saintly mother shone prominently among the ideals that were torturing her like so many firebrands touching her flesh. Oh! how that poor child longed for her mother for the first time during her absence. Oh! that she could sob herself to sleep once more on that bosom that had always been to her as the "shadow of a rock in a weary land." At length she fell into a fitful sleep—crowded, until she awoke, with wild, fantastic dreams. Oh, they were only dreams, so full of charm and delusion. She thought herself walking beside her faithful husband, encouraging him with her love and fidelity. Oh, how she honored him, standing in the forefront as a herald of righteousness! The world, with all its sin and allurement, was forever behind. How her troubled soul was refreshed by those empty dreams! When she awoke, her dreams were rehearsed, but in a few moments they seemed far away in the realm of the unreal.

Tired, care-worn and disgusted, she greeted the gay company in the dining-room. Very soon she was again the queen of that bon-ton resort, and wherever seen was followed by scores of admiring eyes.

One point was settled in Luella's mind: she would consult no one. As to her father's approval, there was no doubt; her mother, she knew, would bitterly oppose the marriage, but she had given her promise, and it must now go ahead at all hazards. She communicated her mind to "Rev. Claude Randall, Pastor of the Plymouth Methodist Church," with as much dignity and formality as though she were writing a gentleman whom she had never met. Dignity and formality, literally translated, often means cold-blooded heartlessness. It was so in this case. Satan can sublimate a heart of love to one of steel, when allowed free access.

Clifford insisted upon an immediate marriage, but in this Luella was firm and would consent to no date earlier than autumn. This disconcerted his plans somewhat, but he knew how well he could afford to wait. And the day was set. The new alliance was not made known in her final letter to Claude, hence, none but they knew of the approaching nuptials.

Two weeks from the night Luella sealed her destiny under the summer arbor, she received the following telegram from her brother John:

"Come on first train. Father is dying rapidly. There is no hope. JOHN."

Mr. Grayson had gone out that day with a party of his own class to a gala-day at the opposite side of the lake. A brief note of explanation awaited him at his room, but the object of his passionate fancy was flying away in another state before he returned. Somehow, she was glad that he was not there to accompany her on that sad journey. Two hours from the time the telegram came, the beautiful landscape of lake and hills was whirling and retreating to the rear like a panoramic vision. Something heavier than lead seemed to hang about her heart; a strange, inexpressible horror would creep over her frame at brief intervals. A dark foreboding seemed to lurk in that one line enclosed in a yellow envelope. Was it devotion to her father? She loved him very kindly, but there never had been the intimacy between them which she always felt ought to exist between parent and child. No, it was not that. Whatever it was that troubled her, it refused to take form, but remained in the background of her imagination to assume more hideous proportions.

Late on the second night, arriving at home, worn and exhausted, she found her father even worse than the message would seem to indicate. He was unconscious, could not speak, and never again knew the faces of his family. The end came soon. Clifford Grayson arrived at Plymouth one day later than Luella, as "accidentally returning home." The funeral passed off with the usual display of many carriages, flowers, mourners, heavily creped, and much eulogy. Dr. Sims preached the sermon. "A great man in Zion has this day fallen. For twenty-five years a 'pillar' in our church. Once elected lay delegate to the General Conference, etc., etc." We can easily imagine about what would be said by such a preacher as Dr. Sims, under such circumstances. The funeral was a great success. Local and even metropolitan papers gave the "untimely death" abundant space. Judge Burbank was cut off suddenly,

New Clothes for the Old Man. 195

and that without remedy. Paralysis of the brain did its work in a few days, defying the skill of the best physicians available. Later developments revealed some startling facts. Why should he be attacked by such a fatal disease? What could have caused such a sudden upheaval in this calm, dignified gentleman, who never seemed to lose his equilibrium. When others were nervous and excited, Judge Burbank was cool. The real status of his financial affairs, he communicated to his attorney on the first day of his illness. Unknown to his family, he had made a heavy investment five years before in a Colorado gold mine. For months he saw the dream of fabulous wealth disappear. His thousands were gone—besides, one assessment after another had been made on the stockholders, sinking deeper shafts, until all his surplus was used up. All this he kept to himself, but underneath a calm, pleasant exterior there throbbed a deep, desperate purpose. Borrowing several thousand dollars on his personal note, he resolved to build up a lost fortune by bidding at the "bucket-shop" business. At first he won, but such winning is only a bait. Many have "won" at first, only to wind up penniless. The Judge's next venture was to borrow on his real estate, as he was unable to make a second borrow on his note, which was renewed at the end of sixty days. The whole story, told in a few words, was that Plymouth's wealthiest man was a bankrupt, and many thousands of dollars of liabilities, beyond the highest value of all his property, consisting of a fine business block and a palatial home. This double calamity, so sudden, and so unexpected, almost prostrated the family. John Burbank had never earned a dollar. Such a thing as labor was the farthest thing in his imagination. He knew no trade, and very little or nothing about business. This startling revelation was a sweet morsel to the gossip-monger. Many were secretly glad of it; many more were truly in sympathy with the unfortunate family. Everything must sell—house, furniture, carriages—as no use could be made of such equipment after the home was gone. Luella refused to see anyone. Her grief and humiliation knew no bounds. The pastor called to speak a word of comfort, but could only send in his card. Mrs. Burbank stood the strain in a remarkable manner. One week before the illness of her husband, she had, through the aid of her pastor and suitable books, received the "white stone" with a name on it that no one knew but she who had received it. The "day star" had risen in her heart.

A new phase in the situation had developed in Luella's case. "They will say I married Clifford because he is rich. If it could only have been known before, but too late now. We have enemies, they will never spare me now." In her heart she almost despised Clifford Grayson and hated his wealth. Her room was almost filled with flowers and silly love-notes from him. For the first time since her last ride with the young minister, she began to see and feel the early harvest of a wicked, impulsive sowing. Never had the noble Christian character of Mr. Randall seemed so true and real as now. He had met the presiding elder's disfavor with kindness and humility, the leading families of his congregation had practically ostracized him. They were simply waiting to be relieved by the Conference, which convened three weeks after Judge Burbank's death. The speech which he was to have made in the ear of the bishop, fortunately, or unfortunately, was never delivered. Somehow, Providence interferes at unexpected times. However, he was to go, notwithstanding he was building up a strong following, but not among the wealthy and influential. Since his great experience he had conducted a great revival in a neighboring town. As a result, calls by the score had come to him from pastors, asking him to hold evangelistic meetings. His duty seemed obvious; for a month he had prayed over this new phase in his commission. To locate and enter the evangelistic field as a "holiness evangelist" meant forever to be separated from his brethren, but he had found it already a lonely way. It promised that at first the price had been paid, and all he now wanted was the will of God, and then follow it at any cost.

After the Burbank household was closed up and everything passed into the hands of new owners, one only sister of Mrs. Burbank pressed her to spend the coming winter with her, in a distant state. This kind invitation she accepted, by force of circumstances. Nothing else seemed to be opened to her. John had secured a minor position with a corps of engineers to go to the southwest, departing a few days after the mother left Plymouth. A careless recklessness seemed to take hold of him since the new order of things, and it was quite evident he would soon be a wreck, as he no longer had the support and protection of a wealthy home behind him. How many, many young men throughout this country would leap from drawing-room respectability to the gutter of infamy, but for the parental influence sustaining them. For John there were no private rooms, furnished with soft carpets and downy bed, to come and go as he chose. No more spending money and club banquets. He faced the hard, cold, merciless world. He had done nothing for it, and in return received nothing The years of supreme indifference were bearing fruit. "Whatsoever a man soweth, that shall he also reap."

Mrs. Burbank left for the East with a heavy heart. Her daughter had communicated her intentions on the day before her departure. To her this was the worst shock of all. The last ray of hope, once so dear, had now vanished. The prophecies she had made some two or three months before, were being rapidly fulfilled. What the end would be she feared even to imagine. Luella was now penniless, as poor as the poorest. She knew better than her daughter the character and disposition of the man whom she was to marry. Such a man was incapable of true and lasting love. They tire of the once beautiful and charming bride as an old garment. Alas, for the foolish daughters and still more foolish mothers who cannot see the dross underneath the glitter; who can not see the beast underneath the latest style of clothing and the immaculate linen, often flashing with blazing jewels.

The Annual Conference was at hand. Many of Rev. Randall's most intimate associates held him at arm's length, while a few sought him out privately to know more of this wonderful experience. Dr. Sims had very little to say to the young man, except a few questions regarding the finances, etc. The conference reached its highest interest, when the bishop was to address the class about to enter into full connection. The usual line of thought about the call and its meaning was discussed by the bishop in an able manner. Oh, how often it is heard, and as often amen-ed, "You are not to choose your field; you are to go, and when a Methodist preacher gets to where he shuns to go, even to the humblest place, where he can preach Christ, it is time for him to quit," etc., etc. At the same time, it goes on, many cases and at every conference, What will the bishop say about our Wesleyan doctrine of "perfect love"? For twenty minutes the conference was thrilled and stirred by an appeal for the old landmarks of Methodism. Not one word was said to which ardent believers in entire sanctification could take exception. Just here is one of the problems that baffle solution. At the bar of every conference, every preacher is pledged to seek, groan and attain; and in the same session, the same bishop does, or allows to be done, some strange, very strange things with the few brethren who claim to have received this "depositum of Methodism," as John Wesley called it. Some of the cleanest and most able men in soul-saving are side-tracked and sent to obscure places. Often told by the elder, "I have no place that will support you," etc., etc. These things are denied, but the fact remains that it is being done in almost every conference.

Again, this *sub-rose* persecution is generally done by men who have not had a real revival in years, whose ministry stands for strict observance to church law, technicalities, collections, and public popularity. We generally find these same brethren high up in secret fraternities, delegates to the grand lodge, responding to a toast at a banquet, where a majority of the gormandizers have no more respect for his religion than the ground they tread.

However, Rev. Claude Randall located and swept away into a broader field, unhindered and untrammeled. In two months after it became known that he had entered the evangelistic field, his slate filled up for more than a year's work. Great manifestations of power attended his meetings. Souls were saved and sanctified by scores. A warm friendship had grown up between Grace Daniels and Mr. Randall during the remaining weeks of the conference; year after they met at the Free Methodist revival. In all their correspondence for months, nothing but the great work of soul-saving was discussed. Her prayers followed him daily. Unconsciously a strong attachment for each other was growing with each communication. "God moves in a mysterious way." He often controls the details of our lives when we least expect it How comforting to believe that the sins and rebellion of people can be overruled for His glory—"All things work together for good."

The wedding of Clifford Grayson and Luella Burbank came off almost without public announcement. It took place in the parlors of the Tremont Hotel. Only a few bon-ton friends were invited. Clifford spent money on the occasion like a diamond magnate. The company was served with six o'clock dinner at twenty-five dollars a plate. The finest claret flowed freely, until the young sports talked a maudling gibberish with thick tongues. Much

New Clothes for the Old Man. 203

of what was said and done shocked and disgusted Luella, but "the die had been cast."

Was she happy on this, the crowning day of earthly joys and hopes? Far from it. A strange, dreadful horror seemed to be settling in her soul, bringing with it hopelessness and real fear. She was only too glad when the hour came for the departure of the parlor-vagabonds. The month of travel and so-called honey-mood was a startling revelation. She was far more hopeless and despondent when they returned than at the beginning. Clifford's dissipated character began to stand out in a blatant manner. Luella could scarcely believe her eyes, when she beheld *her husband* entering the door of their lovely home three nights after their return. Only by grasping a large chiffonier did she keep from falling, in her dazed condition. A still worse fact was revealed some weeks later. Luella, the once queenly daughter of a prominent Methodist family; cultured, educated, the promised bride of a gospel minister, in less than six months, is the wife of a *lecherous drunkard*. Her mother's pleadings and warnings came to her only to mock her wretchedness. In the future she saw poverty as a necessary concomitant of such a life; coupled with it, shame and dishonor. A prophet never pierced the future with a keener vision. A double installment of sin's legacy had fallen.

CHAPTER IV.

The holidays were approaching. Five years and two months had passed since Claude Randall had entered the evangelistic work—going from ocean to ocean, a fire baptized herald of an uttermost Saviour. Five years and one month had passed since Luella Burbank had linked her destiny with that of Clifford Grayson. Volumes might be written about those eventful five years. What a strange mixture of joy, pathos, sorrow and tragedy, if the subjects of the sketch could be followed closely; yet differing in experiences, as widely as it were possible for two souls living in the same land at the same time. Claude and Luella came to the parting of the ways when the crowd scattered and the carriages swept out of the cemetery after the body of Judge Burbank was lowered in the grave. Apparently each had passed out of the other's life. They separated under the shadow of death. That this sad story may not tire the reader we draw a veil over five years of unwritten history, as the experiences of each sank into the realm of deeper consciousness where language fails, and the soul's utterances are comprehended only by the Recording Angel.

Rev. and Mrs. Randall had returned to Plymouth for a rest, and to spend the holidays. Two years before on a bright Christmas morning Grace Daniels became the helpmete of the holiness evangelist. Not only had she found the one man who was above all others to her, but a higher ideal was realized; an untrammeled, unmolested labor for the salvation of souls, the leading of believers into deeper experiences of the Christ life. She longs from the day of her sanctification, to give her whole life to such a work—free from all ecclesiastical rulership. It had all come, and, as she fully believed, as an answer to prayer. During two years she had scarcely seen her widowed mother and sisters. There had been an unceasing strain on their energies for months. Grace had become a strong preacher, taking her place by the side of her husband, preaching, praying, exhorting, and agonizing for souls. The short rest they had promised Mrs. Daniels and themselves was much needed. No place had so much fascination for Claude as Plymouth. The crisis of his life was met and conquered at a a most unexpected time. God had given him in compensation for what seemed to be a great loss—the sweetest, purest woman he had ever met. After it was all over the hand of God was plainly visible in it all. The two had looked forward to the vacation amid the dear old haunts of earlier years.

The first day was spent quietly in doors. It was not known outside the family that the noted evangelist and his wife had arrived at Plymouth as they came on a night train. Early on "Christmas Eve" Claude started for a stroll to look over the scenes of his ambitious pastorate. By chance he passed by the little Free Methodist church, now unused and dilapidated. He went in. The plastering had fallen and the floor and ceiling were covered with broken, deserted homes of "mud-daubers." Cob-webs and dust almost enshrouded the railing and pulpit, where he drank freely of the "Balm of Gilead," on that eventful night. He noted the same pew where he sat by Luella's side for the last time; also the spot where his dear companion had helped him *to go all the way.* Most of the houses in that neighborhood were small frame cottages and old shacks badly out of repair. While he was standing amid ruins and reminiscences, there fell upon his ears a scream, followed by a dreadful calling for help. It seemed to be less than a block away. Any one who has ever heard a woman's cry under dangerous circumstances could never be mistaken. Claude had heard a similar cry of a woman that was being murdered by a drunken husband in a large city. The picture of that awful tragedy came into his mind and his heart almost stopped beating, as he hurried toward the spot from whence the cry came. About a block from the church he saw a coarse, brutal looking man stagger from a miserable looking home, reeling and cursing as he went. The screams and wails were still coming from the open door. Nobody was in sight, but a few ragged, frightened children swarming about, but afraid to venture near. Claude made no effort to recognize the retreating man, but rushed into the house. A sight met him that can not be portrayed by pen. Inside the home was cleanliness, and showed an honest effort at respectability. One room only contained an old wool carpet that had been patched and stitched in many places. Everything was the cheapest, but clean. The woman was raving in a terrible manner. Across her forward was an ugly gash, three or four inches long, which was bleeding dreadfully. The blood was spattered all about the room, and smeared all over her face. Her clothes were torn and scarcely hanging to her body, which showed that a struggle had taken place. The woman was not over thirty—under other conditions would have been good looking. In her arms she held the limp little body of a child; a little girl not more than four years old. She did not notice the man enter, but fondled and kissed and talked to the child between her piercing screams. "Oh, he has killed my darling; she's dead. Oh, how could he?" Then a strange wild gleam would come into her eyes and she would hiss out words, against the man, too terrible to pen. "My child is not dead; she shall not die. I'll kill the man who touches my baby. The villain, the brute! he tried to strike my darling with a chair, but I took the blow." The words came like a torrent. Then consciousness would return and the awful truth came to her again "Oh God, my child, my darling is dead! He tried to kill us both. Oh, if the blow could only have killed me also!" At last the man aroused her sufficiently to get her to hear him, at the same time his heart sank within him and it was by a great struggle that he kept from fainting at what was before him. The child was doubtless dead, and the mother in trying to defend it, had been struck by the demonized father and husband. The woman was too much overcome by grief to notice the gentleman who had suddenly entered and was bathing her face with water and a cloth which he had found in an adjoining room. Presently he called to the oldest boy of a group now gathered near the house. The boy was about twelve and came forward much frightened. "Son, do you know where the police station is?" "Yes, sir," answered the boy quickly.

"Here, take this," dropping a quarter in his hand, "and bring a policeman here as quickly as you can. Now run every jump of the way."

"All right," said the lad, who was almost beside himself at having so much money at one time. It was only a few blocks to the station, and it required but a few minutes to bring an officer, who was unable to get anything definite from the boy's story of what had happened. By the time the officer arrived the woman had swooned, the preacher had laid her on what represented a bed. It was a ghastly sight, indeed. The boy had explained enough to the officer, that no suspicion whatever rested on the man found in the house. It required but a short time for Mr. Randall to explain the whole affair as he had heard and seen. The officer asked him to remain there until he ran to a small grocery store a few blocks away, where he 'phoned for the ambulance and city physician. The news of the tragedy had begun to spread over the town like wild fire. In thirty minutes five hundred people were there, but the dead child, and half dead mother were removed One to the hospital, the other to the undertaker's. Amid the ghastly sight of blood and the excitement caused thereby—also caring for the victims, no thought had been taken of the brute, who had committed the foul deed. As the people gathered a low murmur began, which resembled a growl. The thing was so awful, and so shocking that they could hardly realize the magnitude of the crime. One man touched fire to the dry faggots by shouting: "Where is the infernal scoundrel?" The enquiring crowd was soon transformed into a howling mob. Squads of men started in several directions like so many packs of bloodhounds. As soon as the officers and doctors took charge Claude disappeared out of the crowd, away from the ghastly scene. He left before the name of the family was made known to him. He was overwhelmed by what he

New Clothes for the Old Man. 211

had passed through during the last hour, but had he known who the unfortunate woman was that raved in her blood over a murdered child, the sickening scene would have made it necessary to call the ambulance for him. He staggered into the house, pale as death. The news of a terrible tragedy had gone before him. The whole city of Plymouth was in an uproar. Policemen were hurrying by; men and women were running in every direction. The chief of police ordered the arrest of the drunken man at once, for he noted the danger in the restless, excited crowd. Every saloon and dive was searched by desperate men clamoring for the life of the murderer. The officers were hunting as eagerly with a desire to avoid a second blood-curdling spectacle. What will happen if the officers fail to find him first? What will happen anyhow if he is locked up before these men can taste the pleasures of a crazy revenge? What prison door ever stood against the battering rams of mob-violence? Poor, whiskey-crazed wretch! his doom is certain. The great arm of the state, backed by law, officers, and even a militia, can not stay the hand of fate, when once its iron fingers clasp the throat of its prey. The yuletide festivities of that city were suddenly thrown into a pandemonium;

holiday trade was paralized. Claude and Grace decided to visit the hospital in the afternoon, and if possible comfort the mother lying so near the end of a life of misery. This they did, but were not allowed to see her. Her delirium was followed by a swoon, and each time it was a question whether or not she could rally.

The man was found by a policeman, hiding away in the dark cellar of the vilest haunt in town. It soon dawned upon him that he had better hide away as he felt through his half-sobered brain that the little family row was more serious than he had thought when leaving the house. He had ordered the child to take a bucket and beg some beer for him at the nearest saloon. The mother firmly objected; the child was struck with a heavy stick as it was trying to escape to its mother's arms. We know the rest. Oh God, help the careless, pleasure loving indifferent, so-called Christian people to peep into hovels, in almost every town and city in our broad land, and see this scene duplicated hundreds and even thousands of times. Who can be so dull and blind, and prejudiced and ignorant as for one moment to presume that this land has any other issue of consequence while this red-handed, black-hearted rum traffic is blowing its fumes of death and hell into every

New Clothes for the Old Man. 213

home in the land? It sits enthroned high and lifted up, and blazing with lust laughs to see purity, honor, truth, love, kindness, marriage vows, fidelity, church, God, Christ, hope, faith, heaven, everything noble brought beheaded before it by the gaudy harlot of conscienceless expediency. This monster, more cruel than the Aztec war god, lives and moves, and has its being by the grace of democratic and republican politics; yea by the grace of the Christian sovereignty of this "land of the free and home of the brave," yea by the grace of the Church of Jesus Christ, dominated by men blind in their prejudices and disloyal to their religious vows. An awful deluge of blood is settling down upon this nation that must be answered for, to the last drop—and from the veins of the humblest waif of street or garret. "Woe unto him that buildeth a town with blood and establisheth a city with iniquity."

It was perhaps 3 or 4 oclock in the afternoon before quietness was restored and business resumed. The man landed safely in jail to await his preliminary hearing the following week, but all the afternoon the storm of passion was gathering.

"Well, you're in a box this time," said the jailor as he handed some food through the grate to the prisoner, who by noon was half sober. "W-what 'ave I done?" growling out his reply. "Killed yer wife and chile, that's what."

"That's a lie, an' you know it. When I git out of here, some d— man'll hear from me."

"Yer'll never get out, don't ye worry."

One thing was certain, Christmas festivities would be at a low ebb in Plymouth. Even the sports were chafing for fear their masquerade ball would be a failure because of the intense excitement. Social functions are always the last to suffer. The Martinique disaster never stopped the dancing in Paris. The saloons of Plymouth were uneasy, as strong feeling was already aroused against them because of temperance agitation. They feared that the outraged public would be revenged at their expense. Great care was taken that no man drank until he became drunk. Bill Hobson conducted the worst resort in town. Here the thug element congregated. The wife beaters found their boon companion at "Bill's Place." It was in his cellar the murderer was caught. By a strange intuition he felt that he would certainly reap his share of the indignation. His place had been "spotted" for some time. The chief of police was a straight, clean, Christian man, and the rough element had had any thing but easy going since his appointment. However, it was not the law that caused Bill to close his blinds and lock his doors that day, and place a card outside whereupon was written, "Called away by the death of a relative. This place closed for one week at least." It was plain to all, the meaning of this dodge. It was that or meet a worse fate.

A newsboy came shouting along the street that evening, "All about the murder."

"Get a paper, Claude," said Mrs. Daniels." May be we can find out the particulars."

"Gracious, mother, I know more now than I can get rid of in a month, but I'll get one anyhow."

Claude tossed the paper into her lap and went into another room, where his wife was resting on a lounge. Before he was seated beside her, Mrs. Daniels come into the room. "For goodness sake, read these headlines," she said, holding the paper before them. The name of the unfortunate family had not been known in that home. Claude was too excited to enquire in the morning. He had indistinctly heard the name called but paid no attention, and when asked on his return home in the morning, he could not tell definitely; not dreaming that he had ever heard of them before, their name did not interest him.

To the horror and astonishment of each they read, "Cliff Grayson killed his only child. Wife not expected to live, from a blow on the forehead, etc., etc." Followed by a sketch of the family history, all of which they knew more about than the reporter. But it told the story of his wealth, and who the dying woman was. A belle in Plymouth society a few years before, daughter of Judge Burbank.

It may seem strange that Mrs. Daniels and her family had lost sight of a family once so prominent, but Mrs. Burbank never lived to return to Plymouth, and John was never heard from again. Clifford and Luella left Plymouth, and their return six months before was in poverty and obscurity. It was not known that they were in the city. Only the rough and vicious knew him as he had scarcely seen a soper day in six months. The family circle sat in silence, wiping away tears that stole gently down their cheeks. "Poor Luella, how terrible!" said Grace. "Once so beautiful, so cultured, she never knew a wish denied. We must see that every possible cheer and comfort is given her." Oh, what a torrent of reflections flooded the brain of the evangelist! The past rose,

New Clothes for the Old Man. 217

so real, so vivid, so strange. Across this entire history could be written one word *sin*. Sin paying the last installment, "Sow to the wind and reap a whirlwind." With Luella it had returned a cyclone. Away back through those five years, this once proud young woman had fought and driven from her the gentle One, who was able to calm life's troubled sea. There was no mistake. A thousand times in her lonely hours she had rehearsed that night, when the tempter won the fight and gained her soul, and the door was locked. When they returned to Plymouth, it was she who found the house in that particular neighborhood. It was told that she would take her little child and go into the dilapidated little church and remain for an hour at a time.

At midnight Mrs. Grayson became conscious and called and moaned for the gentleman who came to her rescue. He was 'phoned at once, but when he and his wife arrived she could not speak, but a faint smile spoke her recognition. They bowed by her cot and poured out their souls in prayer. Never did the Shechhinah seem so near. Grace placed her face near the ear of the dying woman, and whispered, "Luella, dear, can you trust Him?" She opened her eyes as a beautiful light came into them. "Oh, such pretty light, and there is my little Pearl. If I could only talk, but it is getting dark. Goodby, I am saved. He has returned." They silently watched the quivering lips, while her poor, troubled soul was being wrenched from its tenement that had known and suffered so much. "Thank God," said the preacher, "since that dark day on Calvary, the dying prayer of sinners can be heard and answered by Him. Oh, His precious blood!"

Luella and her child were placed in one casket and laid away in the cemetery on that beautiful Christmas evening to await the dawn of a bright morn that eye hath not seen, ear hath not heard, nor man hath conceived.

When it was known that a double murder was committed, the restlessness took on a new meaning. The chief of police anticipated the trouble and determined to let the law take its course, by removing the prisoner to another city by night, but the movements about the jail were secretly guarded About 10 o'clock two officers went to the jail and came out with the prisoner and were about to get into a closed carriage, that drove up at that moment, when no less than fifty men rushed upon them and forced the wretch away, hurrying out of town.

New Clothes for the Old Man. 219

In thirty minutes three hundred men were gathered, most of them holding a rope at the end of which was the mangled body of Clifford Grayson. The mob stopped in front of Bill Hobson's saloon. The work was done so silently that nothing was known about it outside of police circles until the next morning. The saloon was a total wreck; not a piece of furniture remained; not a window or drop of liquor, and the body of the dead man left hanging to an improvised scaffold. Sin's Legacy was at last paid in full. The creaking signboard that waved in the chilly wind at the corner of the wrecked saloon, sang a requiem over Satan's triumph at his best.

www.ingramcontent.com/pod-product-compliance
Lightning Source LLC
Chambersburg PA
CBHW031545040426
42452CB00006B/190